D-DAY: 6.6.44

For Saira, who knows a bit about major operations

D-DAY: 6.6.44

THE DRAMATIC STORY OF THE WORLD'S GREATEST INVASION

 THE OFFICIAL BOOK OF THE IMPERIAL WAR MUSEUM EXHIBITION

DAN PARRY

This book is published to accompany the film *D-Day*, produced by Dangerous Films and first broadcast on BBC1 in 2004
Director: Richard Dale
Producer: Tim Bradley
Co-producer: Peter Georgi

First published in 2004

Published by BBC Books, BBC Worldwide Ltd, Woodlands, 80 Wood Lane, London W12 0TT

In association with the Imperial War Museum

ISBN 0 563 52116 3

Commissioning editor: Sally Potter
Project editor: Martin Redfern
Art director: Linda Blakemore
Design: Paul Vater and Hon Lam, sugarfreedesign
Picture researcher: Sarah Hopper
Cartographer: Olive Pearson
Production controller: Kenneth McKay
Project manager for Dangerous Films: Peter Georgi
Picture researcher for Dangerous Films: Jenny Bowers

Set in Rockwell
Printed and bound in Great Britain by Butler & Tanner Ltd, Frome
Colour separations by Radstock Reproductions Ltd, Midsomer Norton

For information on Imperial War Museum D-Day events please visit www.iwm.org.uk

Author's acknowledgements

I am hugely indebted to the veterans named in this book, whose help and contributions over the last two years have been invaluable. It has been a privilege to have been granted access to their memories and stories. It has been no less an honour to speak to the hundreds of veterans whose experiences, for ignoble reasons to do with space, don't appear here. In addition, I'd like to thank Joe Balkoski, Neil Barber, Terry Charman, Stan Cornford, Phil Dolling, Walt Domanski and the Exercise Tiger Foundation, Kevan Elsby, Sidney Goldberg, Colonel John Hughes-Wilson, Major Mike Strong, Lieutenant Colonel Andrew Trelawny, Ron Youngman and all at Dangerous for their enduring patience. I remain solely responsible for any errors in the text.

Producers' acknowledgements

Making a film as ambitious as *D-Day* takes the skills and hard work of a great many people, both in front of the camera and behind. Dangerous Films would like to thank you all; *D-Day* could not exist without you. We would especially like to thank a few key individuals and organizations whose commitment and belief in the project have helped make *D-Day* a reality:

All our highly talented cast, who were often called upon to work in demanding situations. The men and equipment of the Commando Logistic Regiment, Royal Marines, for re-enacting the beach landings; RSM Mac Mckenzie, Royal Marines; military adviser Tony Veale; and Lieutenant Colonel Ben Curry, Royal Marines.

Writer Andrew Bampfield and his script producer Julie Press. Production designer and special effects director Tim Goodchild, whose visual flare is present in every scene. Costume maestros Joe and Yvonne Hobbs, who brought an attention to detail and design second to none. Film editor Peter Parnham, who spent four months turning the mass of rushes into a powerful film.

Mike Kemp and Dan Hall of the BBC's Commercial Agency, whose belief in the project and the team helped to get *D-Day* funded in the first place. The IPM group at BBC Worldwide and especially Amanda Hill for unfaltering faith. Our co-producers: the Discovery Channel and their executive producer, Stephen Reverend; ProSieben in Germany and its head of documentaries, Thomas von Hennet; France 2 and their head of documentaries, Yves Jeanneau; and Telfrance, especially Mireille Sanial, Michelle Podroznik and Sylvie Elmindoro.

We would like to thank the people at Dangerous Films: head of production Jake Lloyd, line producer Bill Leather, researchers Katie Churcher and Dan Parry, production coordinators Christian Fenwick-Clennell and Nicola Instone, production secretary Helen Conlan and runner extraordinaire Robin Chalkley. We would also like to thank BBC independent commissioning editor Adam Kemp, without whose initial passion the film would never have been made.

Most of all, we would like to acknowledge the debt owed to the men and women who fought in the Normandy campaign. We hope that our efforts do justice to their heroism, sacrifice and memory.

FOREWORD

For those of us with no personal memories of 1944, 'D-Day' conjures up a collection of images from films and newsreel, songs and anecdotes from elderly relatives. And behind them a bare historical fact: the dawn attack on the beaches of northern France by 156,000 Allied troops, which marked the beginning of the end of the Second World War in Europe. But for many of those who were actually there it was more than a critical turning point in the war – it was the most significant 24 hours of their lives. For these young men and women, now grown old, the events and experiences of 6 June 1944 are with them every day.

D-Day was the battle the Allies couldn't afford to lose. Factories and dockyards worked to capacity to deliver the enormous resources needed to smash a way into Hitler's Fortress Europe. Every spare landing-craft in the Allies' entire worldwide war effort was mustered for the attack, and more than 2 million servicemen and women took part in the subsequent campaign. The assault itself was so huge, so daring and so crucial that even today the term 'D-Day' is synonymous with any event of 'make-or-break' significance.

The psychological impact on many of the troops who took part led them to bury their memories in the decades that followed. As these men and women enter the final years of their lives, many of them now find themselves reflecting on those experiences and talking about them in depth for the first time. As the number of survivors dwindles and more and more veterans' associations close, the sixtieth anniversary offers them a final chance to share those memories and experiences with younger generations.

The epic BBC film *D-Day*, which shows the scale of their endeavour and the extent of their sacrifice, offers a special opportunity to those who weren't there. Those of us who never witnessed the carnage of Omaha or the massacre at Caen now have an opportunity to share in the lives of those who were there and to spare a moment for those who never made it home from Normandy.

Richard Dale
Director, *D-Day*

D-Day veterans marching in the annual remembrance ceremony held in Bayeux, Normandy

PROLOGUE

By June 1944 much of the population of Europe had been suffering under the shroud of Nazi occupation for four years. During that time every aspect of daily life had been determined by orders from Berlin. In the death camps of Dachau and Buchenwald, in the slave-labour factories dotted across Germany, and in millions of homes from Toulouse to Rotterdam, everywhere hope lay in one form: liberation.

But before freedom could return to Europe there had to be a decisive victory that would give the Allies a firm foothold on the northern shore of the Continent. It was widely hoped that a long-expected attack would eventually punch a hole through the German defences. For many, the thought of a campaign that would sweep the Nazis aside and leave peace in its wake was the stuff of dreams.

From Bayeux to Seattle, the imminent Second Front dominated conversation. In Everett, Washington State, the McCann family knew

15-year-old Eddie would some day be going into action once again, though they had no idea where or when. In Amsterdam 14-year-old Anne Frank had spent almost two years hiding in an annexe behind an office building. For her, and thousands like her, liberation was simply the only alternative to deportation to a concentration camp.

In Britain there wasn't a family who hadn't been touched by the war. Bombing raids, rationing, blackouts, queues and restrictions had been features of life since the first months of fighting. By 1944 most people knew someone who'd received a grim telegram from the War Office bearing news of the death of a loved one. And now the country had come to resemble one giant army camp. Throughout Britain many shared the belief that it was time to take the war to the Germans in a campaign that would finally bring victory and stability. The newspapers said the attack could come any day, but it was hard to know for sure. To all but the privileged few who

People in Britain queue for newspapers reporting news of D-Day

knew the truth, the evening of 5 June was no different from any other.

But in the darkness, 18,000 US and British paratroopers were quietly making their final preparations. Landing in the dead of night, they would be the first to spring the surprise; then, before the Germans had time to react, they would be followed by seaborne landings on a scale never seen before. If the attack was a success, it would be secretly celebrated across the Continent, with relief and joy replacing rumour and speculation … if it was a success. As the paratroopers prepared for action, trepidation and anxiety were felt by most, though few dared to discuss it. There was a common feeling that a job had to be done, and the sooner it was completed, the sooner they could get home.

Aboard boats, ships and landing-craft from Kent to Cornwall, soldiers and sailors tried to find a way of passing the long hours of darkness. Those who weren't playing cards or sleeping were alone with their thoughts. Each man tried to stay on top of things in his own way: experienced officers who felt the weight of responsibility, old hands who'd seen it all before, scared teenagers and everyone in between. Many were trying not to think of anything at all, and a few had premonitions that would prove to be a glimpse of the fatal truth.

After more than four years of war, the tide was about to turn. The garrisons manning the Atlantic Wall, the Nazis' defensive dam against invasion, were about to be tested by the first wave of the 2 million Allied soldiers who were ready to flood into the heartland of Fortress Europe. As Rommel slept, Eisenhower and Montgomery waited for the first news of an enterprise that would make or break the Allies, and fulfil or crush the hopes of the millions of people who'd long been waiting for this moment.

Axis controlled
Allied controlled
neutral

0   100 mi
0   200 km

North Sea

NORWAY   SWEDEN
Oslo•   Stockholr

DENMARK

•Berlin

GREATER
GERMANY

NETHERLANDS

REP. OF
IRELAND

UNITED
KINGDOM

London•

BELGIUM

Prague•

*ATLANTIC
OCEAN*

NORMANDY   •Paris

Vie

FRANCE

SWITZERLAND

•Vichy

ITALY

Corsica   •Rome

PORTUGAL

•Madrid

Sardinia

SPAIN

Mediterranean Sea

Sic

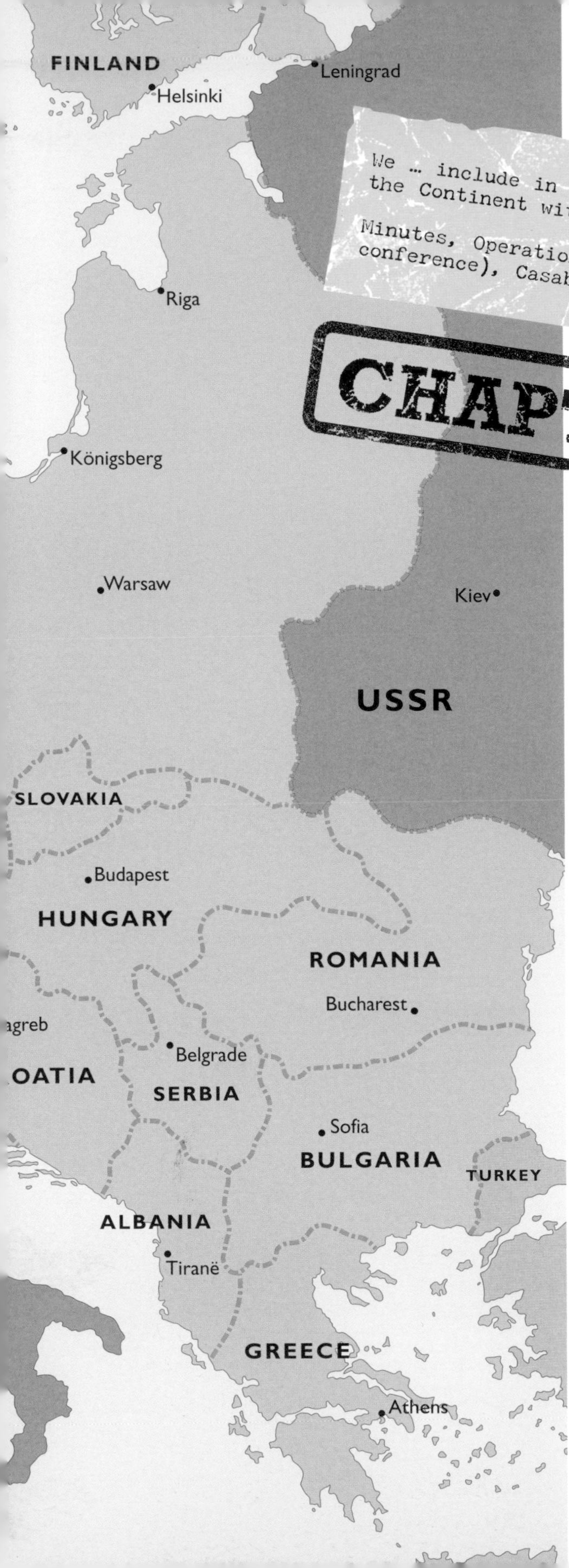

We ... include in this directive provision for a return to the Continent with the forces that will be available

Minutes, Operation Symbol (combined US and UK military conference), Casablanca, 1943

•Riga

•Königsberg

CHAPTER ONE

•Warsaw   Kiev•

USSR

SLOVAKIA

•Budapest

HUNGARY

ROMANIA

Bucharest•

agreb

•Belgrade

OATIA   SERBIA

•Sofia

BULGARIA   TURKEY

ALBANIA

•Tiranë

GREECE

•Athens

OPERATION OVERLORD

The people of Britain had been suffering loss and wartime deprivation since 1939. By early 1944 final victory seemed as elusive as ever. In the east the Russians were steadily defeating German troops, but throughout Europe it was known that another campaign would have to sweep towards Berlin from the west if victory was to be won.

In pubs and shopping queues across Britain speculation about the long-awaited Second Front was rife. By June, after months of preparation, over 2 million men from Britain, the USA and up to a dozen other countries were ready to take part in what would prove to be the single biggest military operation in history.

In the years that followed the First World War a sense of injustice had smouldered throughout Germany as a result of the strict peace settlements imposed on her people. After Adolf

Map of Europe in June 1944 showing the areas controlled by the Allies and the Axis powers

Hitler came to power in 1933, he ignited this frustration into a force for change. Claiming the country needed extra *Lebensraum* (living space), Hitler re-armed Germany ahead of a new military struggle. His blitzkrieg campaigns of 1939 and 1940 carried the Nazis across Europe until a 'Thousand-year Reich' stretched from Poland to the Pyrenees.

In 1939 a British Expeditionary Force (BEF) was sent to the Franco-Belgian border. In May the following year it was forced back to the northern French coast where it was left clinging to the shoreline by its fingertips. Before the Germans could sweep it into the sea, the Royal Navy improvised an emergency rescue fleet. Within days, hundreds of boats were hurriedly sent to pluck 338,000 soldiers from Dunkirk. Its army had been rescued, but Britain had suffered a humiliation.

The British generals began to consider how they might one day decisively roll back the frontiers of the Third Reich. If a port could be captured in a surprise attack, soldiers and supplies could pour into the bridgehead before the Germans had a chance to draw breath. By August 1942 the British, now supported by powerful allies, had decided to mount an experimental amphibious assault. Six thousand men, the vast majority Canadian, mounted an assault on the key French port of Dieppe. Just 2500 returned. Although the raid itself was seen as a failure, it led to the belated realization that ports were too easily defended.

In the middle period of the war neither the British nor the Germans were capable of

Aftermath of the 1942 Allied raid on Dieppe

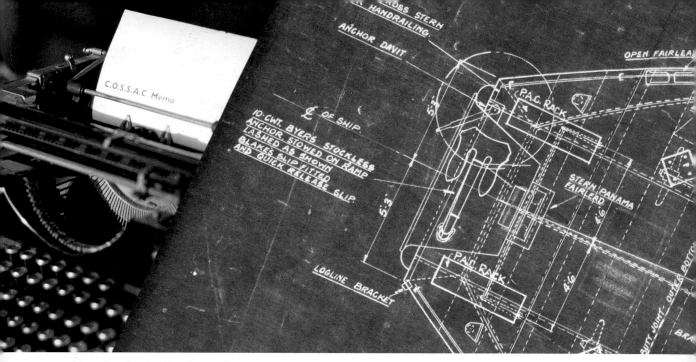

Blueprint of an LCT landing-craft

successfully launching an attack across the English Channel, so attention was diverted to the ongoing struggle in North Africa. In October 1942 British morale was given a welcome lift by General Montgomery's famous success at El Alamein, and for most of the next two years the Allies' victories in Europe were confined to the Mediterranean. But it was no secret that if Germany was to be crushed, battles would have to be won further north, a view strongly supported by the USA. The Americans were anxious to devote their energies to defeating Japan, and since 1941 they had called for a campaign that would bring an early end to the war in Europe.

Following the losses at Dieppe, Prime Minister Winston Churchill initially resisted the idea of a new attack across the Channel. He wanted to focus on the Mediterranean and was reluctant to commit thousands of troops to an entirely new front. In January 1943 Churchill and President Franklin D. Roosevelt met in Casablanca to thrash out a plan for the future of the war. Here the British finally accepted the principle of an invasion in northwest Europe, and agreed to vague proposals

for a 'return to the Continent'. The attack would be planned in London so, with US agreement, the British generals started looking for someone who could begin the first preparations.

Drafting D-Day

Lieutenant General Frederick Morgan was a veteran soldier who had seen the worst of the First World War killing grounds at Ypres and the Somme. Like many senior British generals – not least Montgomery – his experience had convinced him that in battle, lives are spared by amassing enough men and resources to overwhelm the enemy. By early 1943 he found himself planning potential invasions of Sardinia, Spanish Morocco and Sicily. In the event, the first two were dropped, and work on the third was passed to officers in the field.

Although they'd agreed to it, the British were initially uninspired by the idea of a cross-Channel attack. The commander who would lead the actual invasion hadn't yet been named, but at Casablanca it had been decided to appoint someone who would eventually become his

Pre-war postcards of the seaside town of Ouistreham

senior administrative assistant – his chief of staff. There were plenty of capable senior officers serving behind the front line, but the British generals were anxious to avoid depriving the Mediterranean battlefields of a rising star, so they settled on Morgan instead.

In mid-March Morgan was instructed to begin planning another of his potential invasions. Taking the initials of his new title – Chief of Staff to the Supreme Allied Commander – Morgan named his position COSSAC. The term also came to refer to his staff, made up of around 50 officers from Britain, the USA and Canada, who were based in St James's Square in London. At first the British chiefs of staff didn't always regard COSSAC's work as their top priority, but, undaunted, Morgan and his officers began to draft the blueprint of D-Day.

If ports were too well defended, the best alternative was to exploit poorly protected beaches. But which ones? In 1942 a BBC appeal urged the public to dig out any photographs and postcards of the coast of Europe from Norway to the Pyrenees. Millions were sent to the War

Lieutenant General Frederick Morgan

Office, and happy family snaps of children playing at the seaside were studied to see if they also happened to reveal the height of a sea wall or whether a beach had a gentle incline. The pictures led to some early conclusions that were later adopted by Morgan in his own draft proposals, completed by 23 March 1943.

In selecting the target, COSSAC aimed to exploit the Allies' strengths, the greatest of which was air power. Morgan needed a series of beaches that were within the operational reach of

LCTs loaded with men and equipment

fighter aircraft from bases in southern England, that were near each other, and that were broad enough to support thousands of men and vehicles. After examining French Resistance reports and air reconnaissance photos, tide charts and geographical tomes, he found everything pointed to one region: Normandy. The Normandy coastline is sheltered from the worst Atlantic weather by the Cherbourg peninsula, its wide beaches offered suitable exits for vehicles, and beyond them lay ground that could be used for improvised airfields.

The huge numbers of men and resources that would be needed for the surprise attack could potentially be discovered by enemy reconnaissance aircraft. By examining the troops' locations in Britain, the Germans could even

guess the target area and protect it with their best-equipped soldiers. So using an elaborate deception strategy, later code-named Operation Fortitude, COSSAC tried to disguise the Allies' true intentions. Alongside the proposals for the real assault, they began to develop a fictitious plan that focused on Calais, the nearest point on the Continent to Britain and the most logical place to invade. Calais was protected by some of Germany's most powerful tank divisions, ruling it out as a genuine Allied target. But Morgan hoped that if the Germans could be persuaded it was to be attacked, they might keep their strongest units there – and away from other areas, such as Normandy.

In May 1943 Morgan was told that the combined US and British commanders had chosen 1 May the following year as the target date for the assault, which had been code-named Operation Overlord by Churchill himself. By this date Morgan would have to have found all the resources the attack would depend on, especially boats. Troops landing directly on beaches would need huge numbers of flat-bottomed landing-craft, but early on in the planning Morgan was given just 653 LCTs (landing-craft, tanks). On D-Day more than twice this number would be needed.

Morgan was told that fewer than 100,000 soldiers would be available for the early stages of the assault, including 12,000 paratroopers. A year later, 156,000 men took part in the first hours of the operation, including around 18,000 paratroopers. As a direct result of his limited resources, Morgan's plan envisaged just three beaches, compared to the five that were actually used. He knew more of everything was needed, but at the same time he was acutely aware that he lacked the authority to demand it, and repeatedly called for the appointment of a supreme commander.

Once the attack had taken place, thousands of tons of supplies would need to be landed every week to feed and equip the invading army. Since the Allies wouldn't have immediate access to a port, one of Morgan's naval advisers boldly suggested they should take one with them. Using ideas originally discussed in 1942, plans were drawn up for two prefabricated harbours, both the size of Dover. Code-named 'Mulberries', and each consisting of 73 concrete blocks, they would be built in ports throughout the UK, then towed across the Channel before being assembled off the coast of France. One harbour

would support the British and Canadian beaches, the other the American sector.

Supreme Allied commander

In July 1943, Morgan submitted his plan for an attack on Normandy, which was accepted a month later by the US and British chiefs of staff meeting in Quebec, although the proposals for the Mulberry harbours weren't approved until September. The immense building programme that would be involved would have to be completed in record time if they were to be ready for D-Day. Allied commitment to the Mediterranean was still depriving Overlord of much-needed equipment, and neither extra boats nor a supreme commander were quick to appear.

Since US troops would eventually form up to 75 per cent of the ground forces, Morgan knew the eventual commander would be American. By the autumn of 1943 rumours suggested that Overlord would be led by Roosevelt's army chief of staff, General George C. Marshall, who had played a crucial role in developing the strength of the US armed forces. But Roosevelt was extremely reluctant to lose him. Only one other US officer appeared capable of taking on such a huge operation – the Allied commander-in-chief in the Mediterranean, General Dwight D. Eisenhower. In December 1943 Roosevelt met Eisenhower in Tunis and simply told him: 'Ike, you are to command Overlord.'

Britain's hero of the battle of El Alamein, General Sir Bernard Law Montgomery, was given command of Overlord's US and British ground troops. The units to be involved in D-Day would be part of 21 Army Group, and in mid-December Montgomery was made its commander-in-chief.

General Dwight D. Eisenhower

Born in Texas in 1890, the third of seven sons, Dwight David Eisenhower was brought up in Abilene, Kansas. He attended West Point military academy, and during his first posting, in Texas, he met Mamie Geneva Doud, whom he married in 1916. They went on to have two sons Doud Dwight (who died in infancy) and John Sheldon Doud.

Eisenhower served first with an infantry regiment, then various tank battalions before spending the 1920s in staff jobs and the 1930s in the Philippines. During the Second World War he first came to prominence while working for the War Department's General Staff. He was sent to Britain in May 1942, and five months later he commanded Operation Torch, the Allied landings in Algeria and Morocco. As the commander of the Allied forces in the Mediterranean, he went on to direct operations in Tunisia, Sicily and Italy.

Eisenhower's skill at juggling the complex issues and personalities involved in a huge international amphibious assault marked him out as the ideal candidate to lead the biggest military operation of the war. On 7 December 1943, aged 53, he was appointed supreme commander of the Allied Expeditionary Force.

After arriving in London in January 1944, he got to grips with a range of problems, particularly the allocation of resources and the organization and role of the Allied air forces. Ike had to fight to bring both the British and the US bomber squadrons within the scope of his command, and he didn't completely achieve this until 30 March. He then had to find a way of soothing Churchill's fears of high civilian casualties before he was able to use the aircraft to target the French rail infrastructure. This operation, known as the Transportation Plan, seriously disrupted German troop movements.

Eisenhower was a soldier's soldier, and while he knew how to communicate with people, from the prime minister to GIs, he never felt at home with the press. He could not understand their intense interest in him and resented what he regarded as press intrusions. He never accepted the presence of journalists, and sometimes let their work worry and irritate him.

Kay Summersby attaches a pennant to Eisenhower's Cadillac

Monty was a prickly character and his relationship with Eisenhower was not always smooth. Eisenhower's first choice had been the highly respected British commander General Alexander, but he'd been overruled.

However, Ike had been allowed to retain his personal staff, including his driver and assistant, Kay Summersby. A model before the war, Kay first worked for Eisenhower in London in 1942. The two became close friends, sharing stolen moments over lunch at country pubs in between his appointments with generals and politicians. When Ike set up his HQ at Algiers at the end of 1942, he took Kay with him, and there, away from the prying eyes in London, she let herself fall in love. When Ike and Kay flew to Cairo ahead of a conference in Tehran, they sat side by side, daring to hold each other in a crowded but darkened aircraft. 'We were

dreamily content,' Kay later wrote.

At the start of January 1944, Kay – wearing uniforms made by Eisenhower's personal tailor – flew to London from North Africa, along with Montgomery. Monty lost no time in telling the COSSAC staff that their plan was deficient, something they themselves had known for months. He forcibly suggested that their 30-mile front be expanded to 50, and that two extra assault divisions be added. Morgan quickly saw that his authority as chief of staff to the supreme commander had been overtaken by events. When the new commander decided to bring over his own chief of staff, Lieutenant General Walter Bedell Smith, Morgan was given a new job, as Bedell Smith's deputy.

Eisenhower himself returned to the UK on 15 January. Thick fog prevented Kay from collecting

From left to right: Lieutenant General Bradley, Air Chief Marshal Tedder, Admiral Ramsay, General Eisenhower, Air Chief Marshal Leigh-Mallory, General Montgomery, Lieutenant General Bedell Smith in Norfolk House, London, February 1944

him at Prestwick airport in Scotland, so he came to London by train. She knew what a private man he was and wondered how he would settle into his new home near Berkeley Square, squeezed among the area's chattering social hostesses. But within weeks Ike's HQ was moved to Bushy Park in southwest London, allowing him to return to Telegraph Cottage, where he had lived in 1942 and where he and Kay shared happy memories. Here, once again, they could relax playing bridge and walking in the beautiful grounds.

In January 1944 COSSAC was replaced by SHAEF – the Supreme Headquarters of the Allied Expeditionary Force. Along with Eisenhower and Montgomery, its most senior figures included Admiral Sir Bertram Ramsay, who was to command the vast naval element of the invasion. Ramsay had retired in 1938 but was recalled a year later and went on to mastermind the rescue

of the troops stranded at Dunkirk. Commanding the British and US aircraft that were supporting Overlord was Air Chief Marshal Sir Trafford Leigh-Mallory. A clear thinker with a Cambridge degree, Leigh-Mallory wasn't afraid to speak his mind.

Demands made by Eisenhower and Montgomery for more men and a wider front were accepted, and the assault was pushed back a month to around 1 June to give SHAEF time to find extra landing-craft. Time and again Ike was forced to fight for the resources he needed, but he showed admirable patience and determination in his negotiations with politicians and senior military figures on both sides of the Atlantic. Eisenhower might not have had the battlefield reputation of Generals Montgomery or Patton, but in preserving wholehearted international commitment to such a huge operation, he succeeded where many others would have failed.

BIGOT

Copy No ____

Security lapses

COSSAC's plans covering all aspects of Operation Overlord were vast, and maintaining security posed problems from March 1943 right up until D-Day. In September 1943 it was decided that all personnel granted access to top secret documents should be given an ID card stamped with the word 'Bigot', it being assumed that that no one was likely to brag about such a classification. Secret documents were also stamped 'Bigot' and marked with an unmissable red cross.

After Lieutenant General Morgan took over part of Norfolk House in St James's Square, London, he installed a private bar in the building to ensure that his staff could talk freely without risk of being overheard by anyone not attached to COSSAC. But problems still occurred. A copy of the plan blew out of the window at Norfolk House in the summer of 1943 and was handed in by a man who said his eyesight was so bad that he had no idea what it was.

In March 1944 the FBI reported that papers marked 'Bigot' had been discovered in an army mail-sorting office in the USA. The package had been addressed to the US Army's Ordnance Division, but was delivered to a woman who lived in a German suburb of Chicago. A huge security operation eventually found that a clerk had mistakenly sent the documents to his sister.

On 22 April Eisenhower was greatly upset to hear that security had been compromised by a major-general in the US Air Force who'd been a former West Point classmate. Four days earlier the man had offered bets on the date of the invasion during a cocktail party at Claridge's hotel. The officer was demoted and sent home.

Perhaps the most inexplicable security lapse came in May when 'Utah', code-name for one of the invasion beaches, appeared as an answer to a crossword clue in the Daily Telegraph. On 22 May 'Omaha' popped up, 'Overlord' appeared on 27 May, 'Mulberry' on 30 May and 'Neptune' (code-name for the naval aspect of the operation) on 1 June. MI5 cleared the compiler of any wrongdoing, but there has never been a satisfactory explanation for these suspicious 'coincidences'.

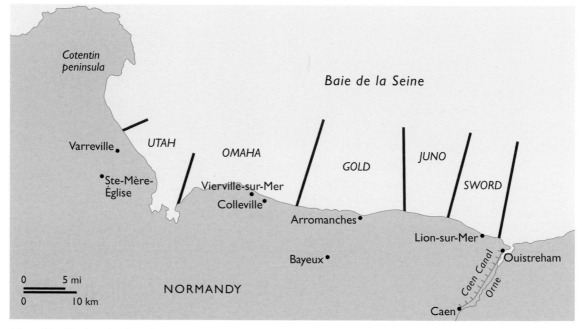

Map of the five invasion beaches

While Eisenhower took on the politicians, the services squabbled among themselves over whether to mount the attack during darkness or daylight, on a high tide or a rising tide, in moonlight or cloud cover. In May Eisenhower ruled that D-Day would fall on 5 June. The rising tide that would come an hour after dawn would allow each successive wave of men to run a shorter distance across the beach than the previous one. It was hoped that this would minimize casualties.

In the months before D-Day, thousands of US and Canadian troops were sent to Britain to join forces with the ever-expanding British Army. The first American soldiers had arrived in 1942, and by March 1944 Americans formed the bulk of the more than 2 million troops from a dozen nations who were in the country. Within 14 days of the landings, it was estimated that the number of GIs in action would be more than double the 1939 size of the entire US Army. Once on enemy territory, they would have to be self-sufficient,

so everything they needed, from engine oil to bandages, plasma to Bangalore torpedoes, would have to be taken with them. After just 36 hours in France the US troops would need to be resupplied with over 300,000 gallons of fresh drinking water.

During April SHAEF authorized the distribution of secret D-Day maps pinpointing five beaches between Varreville and Ouistreham, each of which had been given a code-name: Utah, Omaha, Gold, Juno and Sword. On the western flank, the Americans were due to land on Utah and Omaha, in the middle the British would seize Gold, the Canadians would capture Juno and on the far eastern flank British troops would land on Sword. The code-names for the British beaches had simply been chosen from a list, but the US ones had been hand-picked by their respective commanders. By late May these men were among the select few who knew that the enormous operation was ready to begin.

Field Marshal Erwin Rommel

In June 1944 the Third Reich's western coast stretched 2800 miles from Norway to the Pyrenees. Cinema audiences watching the Nazis' newsreels were told that the cliffs and beaches were superbly defended by the impregnable Atlantic Wall, but this was far from the truth. Throughout the war, the Germans' hardest battles were fought against the Russians on the Eastern Front; the defence of France had never been a major priority. Much of the coastline was guarded by little more than poorly trained, ill-equipped troops manning inadequate defensive structures.

At the end of 1943 Hitler appointed one of the most capable and energetic men under his command to inspect the more vulnerable coasts. From the days when he'd commanded a panzer division in France in 1940, Field Marshal Erwin Rommel had won a reputation for tenacity, imagination and, above all, lightning speed on the battlefield. It was in the open deserts of North Africa that he'd best been able to demonstrate his ability, until beaten by the superior resources of Montgomery at El Alamein.

Rommel believed that an Allied invasion of France was inevitable, as did Hitler himself. But, unlike the Führer, Rommel feared that fighting powerful forces on two separate fronts would lead to the destruction of Germany. However, it was possible that if the Allies were quickly beaten on the beaches, a stalemate would follow. This would allow Germany to negotiate peace in the west, freeing her to tackle the Russians in the east. Germany might even persuade the Allies to join the fight against Stalin's Red Army. To Rommel these were attractive thoughts, but he knew that if Eisenhower was allowed to advance inland, it would

Field Marshal Erwin Rommel

be virtually impossible to defeat the combined might of the USA, Britain and Canada.

While these ideas were running through Rommel's mind, other German officers were contemplating far more dangerous proposals. Like Rommel, they realized that an invasion would leave Germany at the mercy of the Allies in the west. From the Russians they could expect no mercy at all. For these men, the only way to save Germany was to kill Hitler and negotiate with the Allies before the invasion began. These secret ideas were to be developed throughout the months before D-Day.

Defending Normandy

In November 1943, Hitler issued his 51st Directive, decreeing that the German Army's priority was to defeat the coming invasion. On 15 January 1944 Rommel was appointed commander-in-chief of Army Group B, and his duties were extended beyond those of a mere military inspector. In this position he was responsible for the defence of northern France from the Pas de Calais to Rennes: in the middle of this area lay Normandy. Rommel quickly threw himself into visiting unit after unit, and everywhere he lectured soldiers, from generals to corporals,

La Roche-Guyon, the HQ of Rommel's Army Group B

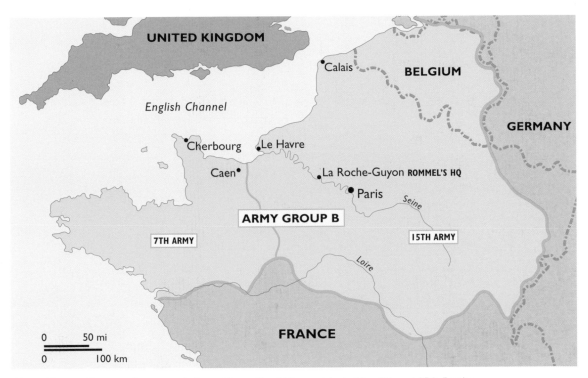

Map of Rommel's area of command, Army Group B, which consisted of the 7th and 15th Armies

on the need to use more gun positions, more landmines and more beach obstacles.

Despite a reputation as a hard taskmaster, Rommel was a popular commander, and gestures such as presenting accordions to the most impressive units endeared him to the men. Although his fame regularly attracted a gaggle of reporters, he remained modest and sympathetic.

In January he visited Wiederstandnest 62, one of several machine-gun fortifications dug into the side of the 100-ft slopes overlooking the 4 miles of beach near Colleville. Unknown to Corporal Franz Gockel, an 18-year-old machine-gunner, the beach had been secretly code-named Omaha by the Allies. Gockel had been living in the post's unfinished concrete bunkers since

October 1943, and he looked on as Rommel angrily demanded that the strongpoint be properly fortified.

In March Rommel moved his HQ from Paris to La Roche-Guyon, an imposing chateau halfway between the capital and the coast. There he entertained other senior commanders as he fought an ongoing political battle. A veteran of armoured warfare, Rommel wanted to keep the six panzer divisions that were in his area near to the coast, where they'd quickly be able to repel an attack. But he was told that the tanks should be held out of reach of enemy naval guns, and gathered further inland, where they could be used in force if the Allies pierced the coastal defences. The invasion was likely to come at

Calais, but it could come elsewhere, and the tanks had to be in a position that would allow them to be sent wherever they were needed.

This argument was supported by the senior commander in France, Field Marshal Gerd von Rundstedt. It was also backed by Berlin. The High Command ruled that Rommel could have influence over only three panzer divisions, the 2nd, 116th and the 21st, but even these wouldn't be under his exclusive command and he'd be restricted in where he could position them. Rommel warned von Rundstedt that the Allies' control of the skies would prevent the tanks moving anywhere in great numbers. He was supported by the many officers who were loyal to him, especially his chief of staff and long-term friend Lieutenant General Dr Hans Speidel.

Speidel was sympathetic towards the anti-Hitler plotters and knew they needed a figurehead. Although Rommel's battlefield reputation made him a particularly strong candidate, he suspected that Hitler the martyr could be as powerful as Hitler the dictator, and he resisted giving the plotters his wholehearted blessing. Throughout the spring of 1944 turmoil brewed in the heartland of the Reich. At the same time, in France, Rommel struggled to find enough landmines, and failed to gain decisive power over the panzer formations. But despite these challenges and uncertainties, Rommel felt he'd be victorious if he was allowed to react swiftly and instinctively the moment the invasion began. Events would deprive him of the chance to know for sure.

Rommel, centre, studying a map of Normandy's coastal defences during an inspection in May 1944

TOP SECRET

Preparations for D-Day (part iv)
Instructions issued to all Resistance groups call for maximum interference
with road, rail and telecommunications upon receipt of the D-Day action
orders from SFHQ.

Eighth monthly progress report from Special Forces HQ, London, April 1944

CHAPTER TWO

THE FRENCH RESISTANCE

In the early months of the war, Poland, Denmark, Norway, Holland, Belgium, Luxembourg and France were quickly overrun in the Nazis' merciless drive through Europe. After France signed an armistice in June 1940, Hitler's forces gathered on the Channel coast, ready to storm their next target: Britain.

The Germans had assembled an army that, at the start of the war, was the strongest in the world. Any Allied attempt to defeat it would take an immense amount of preparation. Until the Allies were ready, subdued populations lived under the frequently harsh conditions of German occupation. For four years grey-uniformed soldiers imposed the will of Berlin. Information, travel and freedom of expression were all restricted. In France a strict 10 p.m. curfew was enforced, businesses were commandeered and homes could be searched at any time. To object was to risk arrest. To fight back was to risk death. The ruins of the village of Oradour-sur-Glane, razed to the ground four days after D-Day with the loss of 642 lives, remain to this day a monument to the brutality of the Nazi regime.

A French Resistance volunteer laying explosive charges

Above: German troops marching through the Arc de Triomphe in 1940
Opposite: French Resistance propaganda poster

Resisting the occupation

Yet, here and there, individuals spurred on by thoughts of freedom and national pride refused to accept the occupation. They searched for subtle ways to fight back, and as the years went by, they became more skilled and more daring. They united into networks and shrouded themselves in secrecy in an attempt to minimize the risk of capture. Collectively they were known as the French Resistance, and their countless networks reached into every corner of the country.

There were many different types of network. Some were simply small, local set-ups; others were affiliated to General de Gaulle; many – such as the *Front National* – had communist sympathies; meanwhile, the more structured groups of the Maquis longed for a general call to arms. Several networks were in touch with the British and French authorities in London, and some were loosely linked to each other. The Nazi security services, popularly known as the Gestapo, tried to stamp out individual groups, and many members were caught and tortured. All volunteers had to overcome a continuous fear of betrayal and arrest as surveillance by the Germans or anonymous denunciation were ever-present dangers.

Salut à la Résistance
—et en avant!

A railway carriage lies balanced on top of a locomotive wrecked by a French Resistance bomb, March 1944

Throughout France the Resistance carried out sabotage attacks designed to interrupt troop movements and disrupt supply lines. Using any weapons they could find, including guns and explosives sent from England, they blew up railway lines, brought down telephone cables, destroyed tunnels and immobilized convoys. London also supplied radio sets and other specialist equipment, along with experts who could teach the volunteers how to use them.

These agents were usually members of the Special Operations Executive, better known as SOE, and they ran great risks in carrying out their work.

When the RAF was ready to drop agents or supplies, the local network would be warned via the BBC. After its evening radio news bulletin the BBC's French service would broadcast a series of what were called personal messages. These were simple sentences that meant nothing to

The Special Operations Executive

In July 1940 Britain's prime minister, Winston Churchill, agreed to allow a new organization, the Special Operations Executive (SOE), to carry out sabotage throughout occupied Europe. SOE's recruits were both military and civilian, they were expected to be fluent in the language of the country they operated in and they had to be prepared to take great risks while acting alone.

The recruits undertook a two-week introductory course before being sent to a variety of different training schools across Britain, most of which were requisitioned manor houses or stately homes. They were instructed in map-reading, sabotage, radio skills, self-defence, surveillance, explosives and small arms, and were given a false identity and a fictional past. They were then ready to be tested, which might involve being woken in the middle of the night and interrogated by men in SS uniforms.

Headed from 1942 to 1946 by Major-General Colin Gubbins, the organization's HQ in London's Baker Street kept track of assignments and agents. Baker Street would give recruits a specific task, which might involve supplying a radio set to a Resistance network or teaching its members how to blow up a German troop-train. Throughout the war F Section (France) sent a total of 470 agents into the field, including 39 female recruits. During the Second World War, SOE was the only British unit that put women in the front line.

Among the most famous was Violette Szabo. She was caught while on her second mission to France, and although interrogated and tortured, she refused to reveal the names of the French Resistance volunteers she'd been working with. She was later sent to Ravensbruck concentration camp, where she was shot, aged just 23. Violette was posthumously awarded the George Cross and the Croix de Guerre for her bravery.

After the war SOE was wound up and its role was assumed by other agencies. In recent years large parts of the organization's history have been released, but much of its work was so sensitive that many of SOE's records still remain under wraps to this day.

anyone who'd not been given access to the pre-arranged codes. They could be heard by people across France, whether they were in the Resistance or not.

Whenever they could, the volunteers hoarded weapons and supplies for the liberation. Maybe the Allies would mount a surprise attack from the south. Maybe they would launch a midnight invasion that would strike at either the Atlantic or the Channel coast, or maybe the Russians would advance so fast that the Third Reich would crumble and the German forces in France would be pulled back across the Rhine. What counted

Robert Douin and reconstructions of the type of sketches he used in compiling his map

was freedom, and it didn't much matter to the volunteers how it came about. So far as they were concerned, any plans for the attack were best left to the generals in London.

By late 1943 the networks in Normandy were ordered to stop carrying out major acts of sabotage that could indicate Allied interest in the area. Instead they were asked to send extra information on the latest German defences and report on whether any anti-aircraft guns had been moved, particularly around Caen – a busy city 8 miles inland from the Channel coast. As the Allies' orders increased, the volunteers in Caen felt one thing was clear – the liberation was approaching.

Gathering information

In November 1940 Robert Douin, seventh-generation artist and sculptor, joined one of the first Resistance groups to begin operating in Caen. Later, while looking for more active work, he was contacted by the Alliance network, which he joined in February 1942. He went on to lead a local branch, and in this position was asked to study the nearby coastal defences. He frequently made secret sketches of German positions before transferring the information to a larger map he was compiling at home.

Douin was also able to exploit his practical skills in his Resistance work. As someone who restored local churches, he was allowed to climb their bell-towers, which gave good views across the countryside. This was invaluable to a map-maker and his masonry sketches would be marked with figures and measurements that in reality had more to do with military structures than with church architecture. Douin's hat, cravat and velour suit, combined with his generosity to the poor, won him a reputation as a local Cyrano de Bergerac figure. His kindness and open-mindedness brought him many friends.

But secretly, by 1943 Douin had become a worried man. He'd been told that the Gestapo were watching him and he was offered the chance to flee with his family to London. Knowing the importance of the map he was working on, and aware that the Allies might one day depend on the information it contained, he refused to leave. For Douin, like all Resistance volunteers, liberation was all that mattered. He continued with his work, and, as he cycled around the region learning what he could, he was assisted by his 13-year-old son Rémy.

Rémy Douin had always been proud of his heroic father, whose left arm had been injured by a grenade while he was fighting for France in the First World War. Rémy had been brought up with what he later called a 'spirit of the home-land', and in October 1940 he cried with anger and frustration when Marshal Pétain called for collaboration with the Germans. Rémy, too young to fight, was delighted when, in 1941, his father quietly confided in him that he'd joined the Resistance. Conscious of his father's past, the boy thought it only logical that he should fight for France again.

On Thursdays and Sundays, the days Rémy wasn't at school, he would join his father on cycle rides, and together they would sneak glimpses of the German defences in the area around Caen. Without his mother knowing, Rémy helped measure the distance between the strongpoints. He and his father did this secretly by cycling slowly between them and counting the number of turns of their pedals.

Hitler's Atlantic Wall

In December 1941, prompted by the Japanese attack on Pearl Harbor, Hitler declared war on the United States. Britain and the USA became powerful allies, and together they had the potential to launch an attack on Fortress Europe from southern England. Dover was just 20 miles from the German garrison at Calais. So, three days after declaring war against Washington, Hitler ordered a defensive stance to be taken along the coast of the Continent.

The length of the Third Reich's 2800-mile coastline from Norway to Spain was to be protected by what became known as the Atlantic Wall. From March 1942 concrete gun emplacements and observation posts were gradually constructed in ports and on cliffs and beaches. Nazi propaganda portrayed the Wall as a continuous impregnable barrier, but in reality it was a hotchpotch of improvised structures.

Thousands of bunkers were built by the civilian Todt Organization, which in June 1944 employed 286,000 workers in France. A total of 17 million cubic yards of concrete and 1.2 million tonnes of steel were used in France, the Netherlands and Belgium, and more than 700 gun batteries were built along the Wall as a whole. The biggest – at Calais – could hit Kent. In between stretched acres of minefields and barbed wire.

The 7800 German soldiers manning the fortifications in Normandy were from the poor-quality 716th Infantry Division, which had its HQ in Caen. Their job was simply to defend the coast, not to launch a counter-attack; this would be left to stronger divisions inland. The division was under strength, and some of its units were made up of Poles or Russians who'd been captured and forced to fight for the Nazis.

By June 1944, some 12,247 of the planned 15,000 fortifications had been completed along the length of the Wall, 500,000 beach obstacles had been built and 6.5 million mines laid. Relying on information from the French Resistance and air reconnaissance pictures, the Allies realized that any attack on France would first have to silence many of the powerful strongpoints. In such an operation, one weapon would be valued above all: surprise.

Devotion to France

Bernard Duval's father had also been wounded in the First World War, and Bernard, like Rémy, was also proud of his country. After the sacrifices his father had made, Bernard couldn't bear to watch France surrender to the Germans. In 1940, aged 15, he took heart from General de Gaulle's belief that his country hadn't lost the war, just the battle. Living in Caen, but not a member of any organized Resistance group, Bernard didn't really know what action he could take against the Germans. Initially, without a word to his parents, he and his friends began to rip down Nazi propaganda posters, replacing them with their own. They later graduated to sabotaging German vehicles, puncturing tyres and stealing radiator caps.

Like his father and grandfather before him, Bernard trained to be a carpenter, but devoted his evenings to art lessons at the art school in Caen. After completing his apprenticeship, he moved to a large workshop, but this had been commandeered by the Germans and occasionally he was asked to work for them. In 1941, for example, he was instructed to make and fit thick, heavy doors for the cells at Caen prison.

Bernard joined the *Front National* Resistance network in January 1942 and was asked to find out what defences the Germans were building near the quiet seaside towns of Lion-sur-Mer, Hermanville and Ouistreham. Memorizing details of the fortifications, he later drew diagrams of what he'd seen and passed them on to a contact who could get them to London. Bernard did this until the end of 1943, when he went to Paris.

Also in Caen was André Heintz. Born in 1920, he spent five months at a grammar school in

Bernard Duval

Bristol when he was 15. After returning home, he finished his education and went on to teach English. Soon after France was invaded, André was approached by a Polish priest, who asked if he was interested in gathering information about German bomber squadrons that were using the airfields around the city. Worried about the fate of his friends in England and humiliated by the presence of the Germans, André agreed to help. He joined the Cahors–Asturie network, and as well as watching airfields, he helped to produce false identity cards for people in trouble – such as Allied airmen who'd crash-landed in the region. Later he helped to distribute

André Heintz

to get the information he wanted was to speak to friends in the tax collector's office. Sometimes they would even be able to give him a precise survey map. Another valuable source of information was gossip. André would go to the bus station and, after joining a queue, would start a casual conversation that he could steer towards news from the surrounding towns.

Serving in secrecy

Later in the war André used to meet the leader of his local network in the church of Saint-Sauveur, where each week he'd be given specific questions about a particular strongpoint or a military unit. André and his contact would each enter the church through a different entrance at 6.30 a.m. and, silently kneeling beside each other during early morning Mass, they would swap prayer books. André's contained the information he'd collected over the previous week, and the other held a new questionnaire that he would take home and study. In the cellar of his house he had hidden a crystal radio set in a tin, and in the evenings he would listen out for the BBC's messages. Although he never told his parents about his work, he suspected they might have guessed.

underground newspapers and pamphlets, which were aimed at keeping up the morale of local people.

André was also involved in discovering which German units had recently moved into the area, and where defensive positions, such as minefields, were being built. Farmers prevented from using a particular field had to inform the local authorities, and he found the quickest way

Resistance volunteer making leaflets in secret

Throughout the war Resistance fighters often left one group for another when the work dried up or if the Gestapo came too close for comfort. André eventually left the Cahors–Asturie network and joined the covert OCM (Civilian and Military Organization). Different groups could operate in the same city as the demand for total secrecy meant it was impossible for a casual observer to know exactly who worked for the Resistance or to which group they belonged.

For example, as well as André Heintz, the members of the OCM included Jacques Vico, who had no idea that his father, Roland, was also a Resistance volunteer. Roland served with Robert Douin, the map-maker. Douin was in fact the director of fine art at the art school in Caen, and among the pupils who attended his evening classes was Bernard Duval, the carpenter who made and hung the doors at Caen prison – but neither Bernard nor Robert knew the other was in the Resistance. It was through the art classes that Bernard also came to know Robert's son, Rémy, who attended on Wednesday and Saturday evenings and was sometimes used by his father as a model. But the secret underground work in which both Rémy and Bernard were involved was never discussed by either of them.

The net tightens

By early 1944 the Gestapo were closing in on the Resistance networks in Normandy. A volunteer from the Caen branch of the *Front National* was arrested and beaten until he named the group's members – including Bernard Duval. On 7 March others were arrested, but Bernard was still in Paris and so escaped capture. Robert Douin knew he was being watched, but he still refused to flee to England, believing he couldn't afford to stop his work. At the end of 1943 he had told his wife for the first time what he was secretly doing, and in early 1944 he sent Rémy, who was in poor health, to stay with relatives in the countryside.

On 9 March Bernard Duval came back from Paris to visit his parents in Caen. It was a grave mistake. At dawn on the 10th two Frenchmen working for the militia came to arrest him. His mother – who had no idea that he belonged to the Resistance – urged him to escape, but Bernard knew that if he was found to be missing, she would be arrested herself. Seeing that the situation was hopeless, he agreed to go with them.

Bernard was taken to the Gestapo's head-quarters and told he'd be shot if he didn't talk. When he insisted he knew nothing, he was handcuffed to a chair and beaten with a rubber club for five hours. Time and again he was called a spy until eventually he was thrown downstairs and bundled into one of the Gestapo's infamous black lorries. His entire body was so badly battered that when he saw someone he knew, his friend failed to recognize him. Bernard was taken to the city's prison and locked in cell 27. The door was one he himself had fitted two years earlier.

Caen prison, as filmed in the BBC D-Day production

On 16 March Robert Douin went to meet a contact at Caen railway station but found no one there. The next day several members of the Alliance network were arrested – including Robert. He too was beaten by the Gestapo, who broke his weakened left arm before taking him to the prison. He spent time in the 'cooler', a punishment room, where he was kept tied up in the dark before being thrown into an ordinary cell. In the cell next door was Bernard Duval, and the two were able to talk to each other through a gap at the top of the wall. Robert managed to write secret letters to his wife by pricking dotted words into pieces of parcel paper which he hid in the laundry basket she collected once a week. Rémy, hidden in the countryside, learnt about his father's fate a few weeks later.

Holding out for the Allies

Like most of the networks in Caen, André Heintz's OCM was regularly asked to supply details about the huge gun batteries that were being built along the coast. Sending information to London by radio was dangerous work. If the transmission lasted longer than nine minutes, the operator's location could be found by the Germans. André's operator, nicknamed the 'Pianist', felt safer in the countryside than in the city, where enemy soldiers moved about in large numbers. Ideally, he liked to transmit while hidden in the depths of a cornfield.

At the beginning of May André was told to learn six coded sentences that would be broadcast by the BBC. The first of these was *'L'heure du combat viendra'* (The time of the fight

Resistance radio operator in action

will come), indicating that the rest would follow in a day or two. These codes would in effect be a call to arms, urging the volunteers to cut railway lines and telegraph cables ahead of the Allies' attack, which would begin within hours. To André his new instructions confirmed one thing – the liberation was on its way at last. Concealing his excitement, he tried to live life as normal.

In Caen prison, when Bernard's cell door suddenly swung open he was terrified to find that a German priest had been sent to him, and believed he was about to be read the last rites.

On the front of the door, Bernard saw the word 'spy' written in German with an exclamation mark. He asked the priest what the exclamation mark meant, but the priest simply muttered 'special case' and asked Bernard if he wanted to pray. Nothing came of this worrying omen and as the days crept by, 19 May arrived and Bernard remembered it was his 19th birthday. The following day he was led out of his cell, chained to other prisoners and taken out of the prison.

Surrounded by SS guards, Bernard believed this would be his last moment. But the German soldiers shouted that he and the other prisoners were lucky and had been chosen for work in Germany. Bernard was pushed on to a lorry and taken to Caen station, and from there he was sent to the Compiègne concentration camp outside Paris.

Meanwhile, Robert Douin and the rest of the Resistance prisoners still inside the prison believed that liberation would come eventually, but realized it was a race against time. Who would get to them first – Allied soldiers or Nazi executioners? While Robert waited, outside the prison André Heintz let himself dream of the day of victory he knew was approaching.

CHAPTER THREE

TRAINING THE TROOPS

Throughout the spring of 1944 Eisenhower, Montgomery and the other senior US and British commanders visited airbases and army camps as often as they could. The troops' training exercises were tailored to each unit's individual role. Paratroopers, for example, practised for their particular D-Day task, whether it be capturing a strategic ridge or destroying a gun battery. Meanwhile, the troops who were due to land by sea were shown how to deal with minefields and enemy machine-gunners.

Eisenhower, his deputy Tedder, and Montgomery inspect troops training for D-Day, February 1944

47

Landing-craft approaching Slapton Sands in Devon during a training exercise

In late 1943 the War Cabinet agreed to the building of an assault training centre on the south Devon coast. Three thousand civilians in six villages were ordered to leave their homes within a month. In mid-December, Royal Navy staff set up offices in the region around Slapton Sands and supervised the evacuation of families who for generations had fished the local waters or farmed the surrounding countryside. The villagers were told they'd be able to return home one day, though no one could say when. After they left, barbed wire was laid out and a 30,000-acre site was declared off limits.

In the early months of 1944 the first full-scale rehearsals for the D-Day landings were being planned. These were designed to bring the men as close to the realities of war as possible, and one of the biggest, Exercise Tiger, began at Slapton Sands in April. It involved all 23,000 of the US soldiers who were preparing to land on Utah Beach. On the 26th the men were taken out into the Channel on landing-ships and the first waves of assault troops stormed the English beach at dawn on the 27th. They encountered simulated machine-gun attacks, and even fake dead bodies.

Twenty-year-old Corporal Jean Cain's unit had been sent aboard an LST (landing-ship, tank).

British assault troops storm a beach from a dummy landing-craft, watched by observers

Known to some of the men as a 'large slow target', the lumbering, flat-bottomed vessels could take 300 soldiers and 60 vehicles straight on to a beach. Their huge bow-doors would creak open, quickly spilling troops and trucks directly on to the sand. Jean knew that aboard one of the other LSTs in his convoy was his twin brother, Jay. The boys were very close and had always stuck together while growing up in Missouri during the tough days of the Depression.

The Cains were both serving in supply units. Their two ships had been joined by six others, and together the eight vessels were just a tiny fraction of the huge fleet taking part in the

exercise. The supply troops, medics and beach engineers in the Cains' small convoy weren't due to land until a day after the main practice assault. Eisenhower would be watching the start of the rehearsal on the 27th, but by the time the Cains arrived on the 28th Ike would be long gone: generals don't stick around to watch support troops. As the driver of an amphibious vehicle with the 3207th Quartermaster Service Company, Jean would be taking all types of supplies from the ships directly to the assault units a mile or so inland. Further down the beach, Jay would be doing the same thing, ferrying everything from bullets to bandages.

Right: Lieutenant Hans Schirren

Above right: Commander Bernard Skahill

Night raid

On the night of the 27th, the Cains' convoy was slowly making its way through Lyme Bay. The eight US vessels were protected by two Royal Navy ships, but owing to an error in the paperwork, the landing-ships and their escorts were on different radio frequencies and couldn't talk to each other. When the destroyer HMS *Scimitar* returned to Plymouth after being lightly rammed, her skipper was unable to inform the Americans. The US officer responsible for the landing ships, Commander Bernard Skahill, was directing the convoy from the bridge of Jean Cain's vessel, LST 515. Once the *Scimitar* left, he had no way of knowing he was being protected only by HMS *Azalea*, a small ship armed with little more than anti-aircraft guns.

Shortly before 2 a.m. the LSTs, inadequately protected and vulnerable, were suddenly discovered by nine E-boats. These motor torpedo boats were among the fastest and most formidable vessels in the German Navy. Screaming across the water, they fired a stream of green tracer shells that sent waves of fear and confusion throughout the convoy. One E-boat released two torpedoes, and moments later a sheet of flame leapt from the landing-ship LST 507. She was fatally damaged, and as she started to sink, some of the 447 soldiers and sailors on board began to throw themselves into the black waters of the Channel.

Skahill saw the flames but had no idea what had happened due to an earlier order for radio silence. Worse was yet to come. At 2.15 a.m. E-boat S-145, under the command of 25-year-old Lieutenant Hans Schirren, was searching for a second target. He teamed up with another boat and together they closed in on Jay Cain's ship.

51

Both fired torpedoes and two slammed into the side of the vessel, LST 531. As she began to list to starboard, the sinking ship was rocked by explosions, and injured men were left screaming for help as they were thrown into pools of oil burning on the surface of the sea. Shortly before 2.30 a.m. Schirren found LST 289; he fired a torpedo and another explosion burst across the Channel. The 289's stern was severely damaged, but her crew were able to keep her afloat.

By 3.30 a.m. Commander Skahill, responsible for the six remaining ships, felt he couldn't risk losing more of his men, so he abandoned his part in the exercise and sent his LSTs back to port. But behind them up to a thousand sailors and soldiers, many wearing full battledress, lay

Corporals Jean and Jay Cain

The damaged stern of LST 289

Coxswain Eddie McCann

Lieutenant Henry Saucier

stranded in the water. Soon the cold began to bite. Hundreds of men had incorrectly fastened their life jackets, and hypothermia, burns and shock were quickly taking their toll.

Going back for the survivors

At around 4 a.m. an argument erupted aboard Skahill's ship, LST 515. The skipper, Lieutenant John Doyle, refused point-blank to abandon the survivors, and after returning to the scene of the attack he summoned Eddie McCann, coxswain of one of the ship's landing-craft. A veteran of three amphibious invasions, McCann was just 15 years old. While growing up in Washington State, he'd worked on fishing-boats before running away at the age of 13. In August 1942 he'd paid a drunk five bucks to pose as his father and bluffed his way into the navy.

With orders to pick up only the living, McCann set off into the darkness and, moving slowly

through bodies and wreckage, he eventually found 45 survivors. At one point while peering into the water he reeled after seeing the disfigured body of Lieutenant Henry Saucier, a friend he'd known since 1942. Saucier had been transferred to LST 507 after losing the toss of a coin.

McCann brought the survivors back to his ship – the same one Jean Cain was on, although Jean didn't yet know what had happened. Throughout 28 April small boats brought the victims to shore and junior officers began the grim task of counting and identifying the bloated bodies. When the toll climbed to 749 dead or missing, only then did the scale of the tragedy become clear. The bodies were taken from the area and hurriedly buried. But they never found Jay Cain. Jean was told of the loss the following day.

For him the days of mindless army routine had come to an end – the horror of war had begun

What went wrong with Exercise Tiger?

Much of the blame for the high death-toll in Exercise Tiger must lie with the Royal Navy staff at Plymouth. The 2-ft hole in the escort ship HMS Scimitar was 12 ft above the waterline. Her skipper asked for permission to return to Skahill's convoy, but was refused. He was told a replacement would be sent instead. By midnight this had still not happened. Eventually, the Royal Navy destroyer HMS Saladin was ordered to join the LSTs, but she was 30 miles away and didn't catch up until after 3 a.m.

In the days after the disaster Commander Skahill admitted that he ought to have broken radio silence as soon as he saw the first explosion to check if the ship was one of his. But in fact he'd thought the vessel wasn't part of his convoy, so an early chance to take evasive action was missed.

An unfortunate series of oversights, which began before the ships even left port, are also to blame. The American LSTs were given incorrect radio frequencies, preventing contact with the Royal Navy. Commander Skahill didn't hear that the Scimitar had been sent back to Plymouth or warnings that German E-boats were in the area.

Two factors directly contributed to the large loss of life. First, many soldiers had not been reminded how to wear their life jackets correctly, and second, the ships were carrying much more fuel than they needed for the exercise, so many of the men in the water suffered terrible burns.

Altogether a total of 337 vessels took part in Tiger, and all were under the command of Admiral Don Moon of the US Navy. At the time of the disaster, Moon's ship USS Bayfield was close to shore and he was too far from the scene of the attack to understand what was happening. Even if he'd known the truth, there was little he could have done about it. Nevertheless, in the days following Tiger he was heavily criticized by senior US Navy figures.

British troops training on Slapton Sands during Exercise Fabius in May 1944

six weeks early. When reports of the attack reached Eisenhower's headquarters it was decided that the disaster had to remain a secret: news of the deaths could destroy morale. Doctors were ordered to ask no questions as a stream of burnt and injured soldiers and sailors arrived at military hospitals. Jean and the rest of the survivors were driven to sealed camps and warned not to breathe a word about what had happened.

Among the missing were 10 men who knew details about where and when the invasion was due to take place, and it was feared that if any had been captured by the E-boat crews, D-Day's vital element of surprise could be lost. Divers were sent to retrieve dog tags until eventually all 10 men were confirmed dead.

Eisenhower's planning staff knew their priority was to focus on the coming invasion, and in the belief that they'd kept the disaster at Slapton Sands under wraps, they were free to concentrate on the next task: another full-scale exercise. This time it would involve the Canadians and the British.

Training for Sword Beach

By late 1943, two-thirds of the British infantry assigned to the Normandy campaign were either volunteers, inexperienced in combat, or recent conscripts who'd been called up since 1939. Many, like 18-year-old privates Bob Littlar and Bill Farmer, had been with their unit for only six months or so. Recruited in March 1943, Littlar was a born leader who had been marked out as a potential officer. Farmer had been working as a labourer and was happy to discover what he regarded as some of the luxuries of army life, including three square meals a day. He was trained to use a Bren gun, one of the main British machine-guns of the period, and consequently held a key position in his unit.

That autumn the 17,000-strong British 3rd Infantry Division was sent to Scotland to begin a tough training regime. Littlar and Farmer had been posted to one of the division's assault units, the 2nd Battalion of the King's Shropshire Light Infantry (KSLI), and they began training at Nairn near

Private (later Sergeant) Bob Littlar   *Private Bill Farmer*   *Captain John Eaves*

Inverness and at other points along the coast.

As the troops practised seizing beaches and towns, they were driven on by the battalion's junior officers. Men such as Major Peter Steel, commanding the KSLI's Y Company, worked hard to bring their soldiers to a peak of physical fitness. Steel, a regular soldier who had joined the army in 1937, was a charismatic and athletic officer who demanded the best results from himself and his men. Always well turned out, he had a memorable sense of humour, but was not a man you'd want to cross.

While the training progressed, landing schedules were worked out and basic details on the enemy were passed down to junior intelligence officers. In the 2nd Battalion of the KSLI this post was held by Lieutenant John Eaves. Like Littlar and Farmer, Eaves had joined in 1943, and was given the job after his battalion commander discovered he could speak French and German. Eaves was a sensitive man who would probably never have joined the army had his country not been at war. But he was a resourceful officer and made the best of his situation.

In April the division was sent south and its troops were assigned to vast sausage camps – so called after their shape on maps. Privates Bob Littlar and Bill Farmer, Major Steel and the newly promoted Captain Eaves were sent to a site hidden in woodland near Haywards Heath, Sussex, and there they began preparing for the latest full-scale rehearsal. Whereas Exercise Tiger included only the troops who were due to land on Utah, Exercise Fabius involved the men who were preparing to attack the other four beaches.

Fabius began on 3 May, and this time the exercise was not spotted by the German Navy. After the men returned to Haywards Heath, the camp was sealed on 13 May. With entry and exit severely restricted, the first secret D-Day briefings could finally begin. The troops still weren't told when the attack would be, but inside heavily guarded tents they were shown real maps of the target areas – although code-names were given to the towns.

Littlar and Farmer were told little more than that they were due to land at somewhere code-named

Lieutenant Colonel Terence Otway.

Queen Beach, which was part of a bigger stretch of coast called Sword. Nearby there were places called Vienna, Tunis and Brazil, and the KSLI's first objective was Poland, a city 8 miles inland. To 18-year-old country lads, it was all very mystifying. Only the battalion commander and one or two others, including Eaves, the intelligence officer, knew the target was actually the city of Caen. Eaves was also told that the tanks of the 21st Panzer Division were moving towards the Caen area, but he was not yet allowed to make this generally known.

The distribution of military-issue French francs and phrase books finally ended any doubt as to which country was to be targeted. The men were also given inflatable lifebelts, 24-hour ration packs, self-heating soups, yellow pennants to identify themselves to aircraft, and waterproof overtrousers. By June 1944, the men of the King's Shropshire Light Infantry had become a strong fighting unit and were ready for action on the Second Front – wherever exactly that would be.

The paratroopers – the first men into battle

While the KSLI and 100,000 other D-Day assault troops were completing their training, elite forces across the UK were preparing for a host of top-secret missions. These forces ranged from the naval interrogation units – specialists in capturing and questioning prisoners – to the Allies' parachute regiments, which were capable of surprise attacks on isolated targets such as bridges. More than 6000 British and 12,000 US soldiers who were due to take part in D-Day would be landing in France either beneath a parachute or in a glider. The airborne battalions, each with around 600 men, were regarded as self-sufficient and given specific tasks behind enemy lines that were aimed at protecting the vulnerable flanks of the bridgehead.

One of the most daring missions of all was the destruction of a powerful gun battery near the village of Merville, on the extreme eastern edge of the entire D-Day operation. Intelligence reports suggested that its huge concrete bunkers contained four 150-mm guns, capable of causing immense damage to the KSLI and other battalions landing on Sword Beach. The site was heavily fortified and surrounded by barbed wire, landmines and an anti-tank ditch. Attacking it would be a formidable task requiring a bold plan and intense training.

On 2 April 1944 the mission was handed to Lieutenant Colonel Terence Otway, the newly appointed commander of the 9th Battalion of Britain's Parachute Regiment. A tough, no-nonsense officer of Irish descent, Otway had served in India and China before taking a staff job in Whitehall. After being given his mission,

Overleaf: Map showing sectors of Sword Beach. The villages inland have been given code-names.

Lisa Grogan

Lieutenant Alan Jefferson

Private Sid Capon

he was locked in a room filled with maps and models of the target and told he couldn't leave until he'd come up with a plan.

Otway produced complicated proposals that involved split-second timing, an array of heavy weapons, experts from other units and gliders crash-landing within the battery compound.

To carry out the mission, Otway knew his soldiers would need intimate knowledge of the target. He couldn't tell them where it was, but he could show them what it looked like. Choosing a hill near West Woodhay in Berkshire, Otway ordered 100 of his men to build a full-scale replica of the battery using timber and hessian, based on details supplied by reconnaissance aircraft and the French Resistance. Even nearby hedges and stiles were faithfully reconstructed to help the troops find their way around the landscape come the night of the attack.

Once the replica was built, the paratroopers were put through a tough training regime that ensured each man was familiar with not only his own job, but those of his mates as well. A platoon of 30 men under Lieutenant Alan Jefferson had

been ordered to lead the assault on the first of the four gun bunkers, known as Number One Casemate. Jefferson's interest in ballet had won him the nickname 'Twinkletoes', and on his occasional weekends off he would race up to London to spend time with the dancers, especially one of the prettiest, a girl called Lisa Grogan. On one occasion Jefferson was able to take his mind off the intense training by appearing in Act II of *Swan Lake* at the People's Palace Theatre in the Mile End Road in London.

Among the soldiers in Jefferson's platoon was 20-year-old Private Sid Capon. A popular Londoner, his role was to find and kill the German gunners in the casemate. By swearing and yelling at the top of his voice, Capon was encouraged to build up his aggression. The men were continually reminded that in the Parachute Regiment you had to be a winner; only winners would survive an operation like this. But Capon took comfort from the thought that he wouldn't be alone – he'd be part of a team and the soldiers would be supporting each other.

Right: Model of Merville Battery

One of Jefferson's closest friends in the battalion was Lieutenant Mike Dowling, another platoon commander. He and Dowling shared the same sense of humour and revelled in reminding each other about the risk of stepping on a landmine at Merville.

It was an ironic way of keeping the prospect of death at bay. They discussed life after the war and both agreed that farming seemed a good option. They even talked about establishing a joint farm abroad, maybe growing oranges.

After spending a month perfecting their skills, the paratroopers had the utmost confidence in their ability to take on the battery. Each man knew the whole plan in intimate detail. A small group would clear a path through the minefields, preparing the way for the three rifle companies – each with fewer than 200 men. At 4.30 a.m. the companies would launch the attack. B Company, which included Lieutenant Dowling, would blow gaps in the wire, allowing the men of C Company, among them Lieutenant Jefferson's platoon, to storm the casemates. At the same time three gliders, each carrying part of A Company, together with Royal Engineers and their explosives, would crash-land directly inside the battery's barbed wire perimeter fence. The whole attack had to be completed before 5.30 a.m. The men knew the Royal Navy would be waiting for a signal indicating that the mission had been successful. If none came, HMS *Arethusa*, waiting offshore, would begin a heavy bombardment, and anyone still in the area wouldn't stand a chance.

Ready for action

The paratroopers had prepared for each phase of the assault down to the finest detail. After nine major rehearsals, including four at night, they were taken back to their barracks in Wiltshire, where Lieutenant Colonel Otway told his officers that after destroying the fortified gun position, the men would attack a nearby radar station. As instructed, Lieutenant Jefferson briefed his soldiers about Merville, then he too mentioned the radar station.

But unknown to Jefferson, a corporal from the Security Investigation Bureau had been planted in his platoon by Otway, who didn't have the same confidence in Jefferson that he had in some of his other officers. The corporal appeared to be simply a regular paratrooper, but following his secret orders, he informed Otway about Jefferson's reference to the radar station. The colonel was furious. He told Jefferson that this information had been meant for officers only, and that by telling his men he'd compromised security. Otway warned him that normally he would have been taken off the operation, but Jefferson couldn't be spared, so the matter was dropped.

At the end of May the men were transferred to RAF Broadwell in Oxfordshire, where they were given their final operational briefing. It was from here that they would eventually leave for France, and it was here that the nerves first set in. All that the men of the 9th Parachute Battalion needed now was good weather and a little luck. Both proved to be in short supply.

Preparing the paratroopers

Before they began training for their attack on the Merville Battery, the men of the 9th Parachute Battalion worked hard to build up their fitness. This involved tackling assault courses and completing timed runs, which often took place just an hour or so before a period of leave was due to begin. Only those who finished on time would catch the express to London. Everybody else would be stuck on the slow train.

On one occasion Private Capon and a couple of his mates appeared before their company commander in vests and shorts and asked permission to go on a run. Capon and the others promptly ran out of the camp and into a pub, where they sat down to a pint or two. After a while the officer came into the same pub, but on seeing the men, he merely smiled and asked if they'd like another drink.

Initiative and a sense of independence were encouraged in the Parachute Regiment. Since the men would be fighting behind enemy lines, they had to be more resourceful than soldiers in regular infantry units. This meant they needed to be able to deal with all types of situation. While they were at West Woodhay, this was put to the test by Lieutenant Colonel Otway.

Earlier in the war Otway had held a staff job in Whitehall, and his responsibilities included occasionally briefing Churchill on secret plans. The sensitive nature of the work required him to take security extremely seriously. He was, for example, forbidden to read newspapers, so that when chatting about the war with friends he would be sure the things he knew could have come only from secret reports and were not to be discussed.

Having been given his top-secret D-Day mission, Otway continued to regard security as an essential part of his job. To be certain his men wouldn't let him down, he once sent 30 of the prettiest members of the Women's Auxiliary Air Force, in civilian clothes, into village pubs near where the soldiers were training. They were asked to do all they could to discover the men's mission, but the troops passed the test and gave nothing away.

Deployment orders, Operation Tarbrush, 13 May 1944
Not to be allowed to fall into the hands of the enemy.
To be destroyed on completion.
INTENTION: To obtain a beach mine from the enemy-
defended coast, to obtain information of the nature
of beach defences, and to withdraw unobserved.

CHAPTER FOUR

SEARCHING FOR SECRETS

From March 1944, British newspapers published countless stories speculating on the imminent Second Front. Eisenhower's appointment was widely reported, and one magazine even devoted seven pages of pictures to the Grosvenor Square offices earmarked for the supreme commander. By the time Ike briefed his senior officers at St Paul's School in London on 15 May, more than 100 journalists representing newspapers and news agencies from both sides of the Atlantic were accredited to SHAEF.

A year earlier, while Lieutenant General Morgan was still getting to grips with his new job, the Reuters news agency had just taken on Doon Campbell, a young reporter from Scotland.

Devastation at Monte Cassino

Doon Campbell

Born in 1920, Campbell's childhood was shaped by the fact that he was born without a left arm and by the loss of his mother when he was two. At an early age he settled on a career in journalism, and was first offered work with Reuters in April 1943. Later that year Campbell was sent to Italy, and by February 1944 he was filing well-received stories from the bitter fighting at Monte Cassino.

That spring, when Campbell was brought back to Britain to cover the inevitable attack on northwest Europe, he knew he was about to embark on the biggest story of his career so far. But while waiting in London for news of his latest front-line assignment, he was told by his editor that this time he'd be accompanying only the reserve forces. It was a disappointing blow. On 16 May all the reporters who'd be covering the campaign were summoned to a briefing by General Montgomery, and Campbell saw that he was one of the youngest there.

The briefing was accompanied by stern warnings not to report anything until the troops had landed in France. Campbell wrote up almost every word Monty spoke and wondered when, if ever, his report would be published. Like all

reporters, he was anxious to deliver a scoop, but in the weeks before D-Day nothing was happening – or at least nothing that he was being told about.

Shooting the war

By early April another war correspondent, a photographer, had also returned to London from Italy. Robert Capa had made his name during the Spanish Civil War in 1936, and had lived a fast and furious life ever since. Capa came from Hungary, but had spent much time in Paris before travelling to New York in 1939. It was there that he met John Morris, a picture editor at *Life* magazine. Two years later, when *Life* sent Morris to California, he was joined by Capa, and together the pair enjoyed the Hollywood high life. When the USA entered the war Capa tried to get himself accredited to the military, and was eventually sent on an assignment to Europe in April 1942.

In February 1943, while covering the Home Front in England, Capa met Elaine Justin, whom he came to know as 'Pinky'. A month later Pinky saw him off at Euston station as he caught the train to Glasgow, from where he was due to sail for the front line in North Africa. It was there that Capa first met troops of the US 1st Infantry Division, and he would later come across them again in Sicily. By the time Capa returned to London in April 1944 he was a photographer of world renown, who'd been capturing images of war for eight years.

Capa later wrote that London in the spring of 1944 was gripped by invasion fever. Amid the uncertainties of wartime, both civilians and soldiers lived life to the full, and while, all around him, short-lived relationships blossomed in the long summer evenings, Capa devoted himself to

Left: Robert Capa

poker. He played endless card games with famous friends, including the writers John Steinbeck and Ernest Hemingway, and the film director George Stevens. John Morris had been sent to Britain in October 1943 as *Life*'s London picture editor, and together he and Capa made the most of their generous expense accounts, eating and drinking in the pubs and restaurants of Soho and Covent Garden.

As he waited for an assignment with the troops who'd be spearheading the Second Front, Capa renewed his steamy relationship with Pinky, who'd hired a luxurious apartment for the pair of them at 26 Belgrave Square. Knowing that the day he returned to action could be his last, Capa threw an End-of-the-World party on 24 May, and Morris and the rest of the guests put the war on hold as they drank whisky and punch until dawn. Four days later Capa was ordered to go to Weymouth in Dorset to join the unit he'd been assigned to – once again he'd be with the troops of the US 1st Infantry Division.

Doon Campbell and Robert Capa both tried to dig beyond the official briefings given by the generals – who were themselves anxiously trying to discover all they could about the Germans' defences. But neither Campbell nor Capa knew about the new German secret weapon the Allies believed they'd seen. Nor did they know that on 16 May, while Campbell was being briefed by Montgomery, commandos were preparing to capture it.

Operation Tarbrush

Covert missions supporting Operation Overlord were first discussed in August 1943, and that summer, and again in December and January, highly trained commandos carried out daring midnight raids on the coast of northern France. They took infrared photographs, collected soil samples, retrieved chunks of beach obstacles and captured prisoners for interrogation. In early 1944 SHAEF stopped missions to the French coast, fearing that as D-Day approached they risked exposing the target beaches.

But just six weeks before D-Day an air reconnaissance film took the Allies by surprise. Aircraft had been attacking targets near Calais, and some of their bombs had fallen in the sea, detonating a chain of mysterious underwater explosions. The pictures suggested that the Germans had developed a new type of highly

The Allies' foreign commando troops

The strangest of all the Allies' elite forces was 3 Troop, a commando unit so secret that it was originally known only as X Troop. It was made up exclusively of Germans, Austrians, Danes, Czechs, Greeks and Hungarians, many of whom were Jewish.

The unit came into being after the Chief of Combined Operations, Lord Louis Mountbatten, supported suggestions that better use could be made of the foreign nationals serving in Britain's armed forces. Many wanted to join the commandos but were refused permission, and instead were consigned to pioneer units, doing little more than building roads and digging latrines.

In 1942 Mountbatten set up 10 (Inter-Allied) Commando, with individual units made up of men from one country. There was one each from the Netherlands, Belgium, Yugoslavia, Poland, Norway, and two from France, and together they were stationed in North Wales. It was there that in July 1942 Captain Bryan Hilton Jones, a tough Welshman with a fondness for mountain-climbing, brought eight recruits for the latest - multinational - unit: 3 Troop.

Hilton Jones was assisted by Georgi Lanyi, then a sergeant with a background in SOE. Together they interviewed hundreds of men, and a second group of soldiers was sent to Aberdovey in October 1942, with more arriving in February and April 1943. They became experts in parachuting, small-boat handling, explosives, cliff-climbing and lock-picking - skills that made them especially suitable for covert missions.

Lanyi was the first man from the unit to become an officer, and after changing his name to George Lane - all members of 3 Troop were required to adopt false identities - he was ready to take part in his first mission. The unit was involved in the Operation Forfar raids, carried out between July and September 1943, and the Operation Hardtack missions undertaken in December. These were designed to gather information about the French coast, ahead of D-Day, and they demonstrated the calibre of troops who were risking more than the average soldier. Each man knew that if he was caught and identified, his family, still in occupied Europe, would face arrest and possible torture.

Motor torpedo boat, as used on secret commando raids

sensitive mine, so despite the ban on small raids, senior naval and army commanders asked for a closer inspection.

A series of missions code-named Operation Tarbrush were planned to take place over the next dark period. They would be carried out by men who weren't simply a product of their training, but were volunteers whose tough personalities and unswerving commitment marked them out as more able than the average soldier. Among them was 29-year-old Lieutenant George Lane, who had come from his native Hungary under his original name Georgi Lanyi. In the 1930s he had been an Olympic water-polo player, before deciding he wanted to see more of the world. He studied for a while at Oxford University and then became a journalist. At the outbreak of war Lanyi's nationality barred him from serving in a British infantry regiment, but he was eventually recruited into SOE, the secret

organization that specialized in covert sabotage. Sent to France, he trained the Resistance in the use of explosives. He later played a key role in setting up a secret commando troop, which to this day remains one of the least-known elite units of the Second World War.

Part of 10 (Inter-Allied) Commando, 3 Troop consisted exclusively of men from occupied Europe. To mask their true identities, its members were given false names. Lanyi opted for Smith, but settled on Lane when ordered to choose something he could pronounce. In mid-May 1944, Lieutenant Lane was briefed on the Germans' new mine, and he began to prepare for what would be his fourth mission to occupied France.

Operation Tarbrush targeted four areas off the enemy coast, all well away from the invasion beaches. On the night of 15 May, Tarbrush 10, the team commanded by Lane, examined the shoreline south of their target area at Onival, near Dieppe. After Lane returned to England, his senior officers leapt away in alarm when he dutifully presented them with a mine. It had once been a standard landmine, but after months in sea water it had corroded to the point where it could explode at any minute. Mines of this type had probably caused the blasts near Calais, which had been seen in the air reconnaissance film. In fact, there was no new type of mine at all, but the Allies didn't yet know this. On the night of the 16th, as Doon Campbell typed up his notes from Montgomery's briefing, Lane quietly returned to the French coast. This time he was forced back by bad weather.

On the 17th he tried to reach his target area for a third time. With him was Lieutenant Roy Wooldridge, a volunteer from the Royal Engineers, whose expertise in mines had won him a Military Cross at El Alamein, and who'd been called back for this mission from his honeymoon. The team crossed the Channel in a motor torpedo boat before rowing ashore in a rubber dinghy. On reaching the beach, Lane and Wooldridge told the two NCOs accompanying them to wait beside the dinghy until 3 a.m., then they crept away into the darkness.

The officers were delayed after being spotted by an enemy patrol, and by the time they eventually returned, the NCOs, as ordered, had gone. They had swum to a small boat moored at sea, leaving the dinghy behind. Lane and Wooldridge now dragged it towards the surf and rowed out into the Channel. By dawn they'd not got far, and were arrested by German soldiers aboard a motor boat.

Interrogation and conversation

The captured officers were interrogated at different places for two days until eventually Lane was warned that he was going to meet someone very important. Having been spared torture at the hands of the SS and Gestapo – if only temporarily – he suddenly found himself being ushered into the imposing library at La Roche-Guyon, which was being used as an office by Rommel.

The field marshal always liked to question prisoners, and walking the length of the room, he told Lane to sit down. He asked if Lane was one of those 'gangster commandos' and a 'saboteur'? Speaking in a Welsh accent to disguise his Hungarian origin, Lane told the interpreter that Rommel wouldn't have invited him to talk if he was seriously regarded as a saboteur. 'You regard this as an invitation?' laughed the field marshal. 'Certainly,' replied Lane, 'and a great honour.' The atmosphere lightened, and when Lane was asked about the invasion he answered that he knew only what he'd read in *The Times*. Rommel said he already had that information: he received a copy of *The Times* every day from Lisbon.

Lane felt that in different circumstances Rommel would have been instantly warm and welcoming. He believed the conversation was going well, and, anxious to prolong it, asked if he might pose a few questions of his own. Lane asked whether an army could successfully govern a hostile country it had conquered, and Rommel replied that the French people were happy, as Lane could see for himself. Lane said he'd seen nothing because he'd been made to wear a blindfold. After checking with his staff, Rommel was told that this could not be avoided because Lane was dangerous.

Wooldridge was also brought before Rommel, but gave nothing more than his name, rank and number. Both he and Lane were later driven to a prison in Paris, where they heard screaming from other cells though they themselves were not ill-

Lieutenant George Lane's 1944 PoW identity card

treated. Lane believes that Rommel intervened on their behalf, ensuring their lives were spared. Both were sent to a prisoner-of-war camp, where Lane revealed to British officers the details of his extraordinary conversation with the commander of Army Group B.

As well as missions such as George Lane's, commandos also carried out raids to support the Allies' deception programme. Nuisance attacks on beaches well away from Normandy were aimed at showing that the Allies were examining many places along the coast. At the same time, in Britain, rubber tanks, dummy landing-craft, false radio signals and real but empty military camps were used to suggest there were more troops in the country than actually existed. This was a key part of the deception plan code-named Operation Fortitude, and nothing played a more significant role in this than the top-secret work of the Twenty Committee.

Garbo, the master spy

The fake tanks and camps were put on show for the benefit of German reconnaissance aircraft. But by 1944 few of these were operational above England. In fact, the Germans would have known very little of what was happening in Britain at all had it not been for the stories sent back by their elaborate network of spies. By far the most successful of these was the agent code-named Arabel, whose 24 sub-agents were scattered across the length and breadth of Britain. Arabel, a Spaniard, sent radio messages to German intelligence officers in Madrid, who passed them on to Berlin. Relevant information was in turn sent via Paris to Rommel. Well informed and fanatically devoted to his cause, Arabel told the Germans all he knew. He told them the Allies intended to attack Norway and Calais.

Arabel's real name was Juan Pujol, and he was in fact a double agent, working for two masters at once. While being paid by the Germans, who

believed he'd smuggled himself from Spain to London, he was actually ideologically committed to the Allies, who'd flown him to Plymouth in 1942. They'd given him a house in the London suburb of Hendon, and an office in St James's, where he invented non-existent sub-agents under the watchful eye of his MI5 case officer, Tomás Harris. He and Harris were on first-name terms, but to the MI5 spymasters, Pujol was code-named 'Garbo'.

MI5 ran many such agents, and a loose inter-service group decided the role each should play. These men, masters in the art of double-crossing the Germans, named themselves the Twenty Committee, since in Roman numerals a double cross – XX – represents the number 20. Chaired by John Masterman, an MI5 officer who had previously been both an Oxford don and a Wimbledon tennis player, the committee met throughout most of the war. In late 1943 they decided that the best of the dozens of enemy spies they secretly controlled should play a significant part in the Operation Fortitude deception plan.

These agents would send back false information that would encourage the Germans to believe three things. First, that the Allies were targeting Norway and Calais; second, that there would be

Right: Dummy Mustang fighter aircraft
Below: Fake tank

Juan Pujol, master spy

Juan Pujol's double-edged story of apparent fanatical devotion is all the more remarkable for the fact that he was someone who rejected extremism. Born in 1912 in Barcelona, he grew up in a country dominated by revolutionary political views, which culminated in civil war. Pujol opposed the fascist regime that followed and yearned to 'do something practical' to help bring about a more moderate political system.

In 1940, as Europe descended into war, he and his wife Aracelli discussed how he might serve the enemy of fascism - Britain. In January 1941 Aracelli offered her husband's services to the British Consulate but was turned down. Pujol realized he would have to offer something to the Allies, so he approached the German Embassy in Madrid. After he told them he was able to get to London they took him on as a spy.

In fact, Pujol went to Portugal, where he failed several times to win the support of the British in Lisbon. Undaunted, he entered a fantasy world of fiction and invention, and told the Germans in July 1941 that he'd reached London. Although he spoke no English, he knew some French, and using a French-English dictionary, supported by newspapers and the local library, he made up reports of life in England. These contained occasional glaring errors such as the suggestion that there were men in Glasgow who would do anything for a litre of wine.

Nevertheless, Pujol's information was so interesting to the Germans in Madrid that they radioed his reports to Berlin. These were intercepted by the British, who had cracked the Germans' military cyphers. MI5 were informed about an enemy agent controlled by Madrid at the same time as they were told by British intelligence officials that there was a Spaniard in Lisbon who was duping the Germans. MI5 put two and two together and flew Pujol to England in April 1942.

He immediately hit it off with his MI5 case officer, Tomás Harris, himself of part-Spanish origin. Harris helped Pujol - now code-named 'Garbo' by the British - to become the Allies' top double agent. It was later discovered that their work had encouraged the Germans to overestimate the number of Allied divisions by 50 per cent, and it has been argued that if one person had a claim to shortening the war, it was Garbo.

no assault until July; and third, that an attack on Calais might be preceded by a smaller diversion. If somewhere else were attacked first – Normandy, for example – Calais might still be targeted later by the rest of the soldiers dotted around the UK. The spies' exaggerated claims about vast numbers of troops were supported by the extra resources that the Germans could potentially see for themselves, such as the fake camps and tanks. Together the various parts of the deception plan would persuade the Germans that the Allies were strong enough to invade more than one location.

In February 1944 the committee decided that much of this work should fall to the three agents most trusted by the Germans. Top of the list was Garbo. At first Harris feared that Garbo's entirely fictitious network might be too vulnerable to be used in this way, but he eventually relented, and between January and D-Day the Spaniard sent more than 500 messages. To maintain his credibility, some of the information was true, but most wasn't. Using details supplied by the Twenty Committee and writing in a flowery, Catalan style of prose, Garbo compiled reports supposedly based on notes received from his fictitious sub-agents. The messages were then transcribed into

coded groups of letters before being sent to the Germans in Madrid by an MI5 radio operator.

Preparing the bait
Garbo worked hard to suggest that the Allied armies were being held in southeast England and in Scotland – in keeping with the supposed plan to attack Calais and Norway. The work was risky. If the Germans stopped believing him,

there was the danger that they might start reading his messages in reverse and begin to suspect that Calais wasn't the true target. However, the more verbose, demanding and extreme Garbo was with the Germans, the more the Germans learnt not to dare upset their priceless asset by not trusting him. The trick worked: his reports were never doubted.

In the weeks before the invasion Garbo 'moved' some of his fictional agents into better positions, where they'd be able to see the troop-ships leaving port. Some were supposedly keeping watch on the non-existent British Fourth Army based in Scotland, while others monitored the First United States Army Group (FUSAG), in Sussex and East Anglia. Garbo told Madrid that

Agent Number 4, a Gibraltarian waiter working in military canteens, had got himself sent to the Hiltingbury Camp in Hampshire, where he could watch the Canadian 3rd Infantry Division.

On 30 April 1944 Garbo reported that Agent 4 had seen the troops being given vomit bags and lifebelts in preparation for a voyage at sea. On 4 May Garbo reported that Agent 4 had seen the Canadian troops leave Hiltingbury with orders to embark at Southampton. On the 5th he increased the tension still further by saying that the soldiers, now aboard their ships, 'must be moving towards their far-off objective'.

But on 7 May Garbo sent a despairing message to Madrid, saying Agent 4 had 'displayed the ability of a simpleton'. Far from being in the middle of the Channel, the Canadians had returned to camp! They had simply taken part in a short rehearsal.

Garbo's report, filled with disappointment, revealed that he no longer trusted his mistaken agent. He told the Germans: 'In future [Agent 4] will make no further comments to influence me. I am afraid he is a little discouraged by his great stupidity.' This was the bait for an elaborate trap.

As Garbo and Harris had hoped, the Germans were gravely worried by this turn of events. They believed Agent 4 had been working with Garbo since 1942 and was now watching assault troops in an excellent location. They couldn't afford to miss out on his reports, so on 8 May they urged Garbo to reconsider and give Agent 4 'encouragement, as if not, it might happen that when the real invasion is about to take place he will not notify this owing to over-precaution'. The Germans were now anxiously emphasizing that they still wanted to hear Agent 4's reports, and were all too keen to know what he had to say. The trap was set.

Reeling them in

In early June Garbo persuaded the Germans that the Allied troops were ready for action and that they should be listening for his messages beyond 11 p.m., the time Madrid normally went off air. This was designed to allow him to send a truthful – and consequently controversial – warning just a few hours before the invasion began, telling them that an attack was imminent. This message would be received by the Germans just a little too late to allow them to take any action but it would greatly enhance Garbo's already cast-iron reputation. He decided this report would be based on information from Agent 4.

In this way Garbo's credibility with the Germans would be at its highest just when thousands of Allied troops would be scrambling across the beaches. Garbo would then exploit this credibility in a move designed to protect the vulnerable troops. He would warn the Germans that the assault in Normandy was *an* invasion, but not *the* invasion, and that Calais was still a potential target. The trap would be sprung. At the critical moment Garbo's message would encourage the Germans to keep their formidable panzer divisions in Calais and well away from the actual battlefield.

While suggesting a false picture, Garbo also tried to hide what was really happening. He claimed, for example, that Agent 7(5) had failed to set himself up in Exeter due to tight security, so there was now no one who could send information from the West Country. In this way, Garbo was able to avoid telling Madrid about an area where large numbers of US soldiers were actually based. To seal this point, Garbo reported on 2 June that, fictional though he was, Agent 7(5) had been arrested and jailed for breaching security restrictions.

If Operation Fortitude failed, there'd be every possibility that the German divisions in Calais would be sent to Normandy before the Allies had landed enough of their own tanks to deal with them. In working to prevent this, MI5's top double agent played a crucial role. It was later discovered that on 15 May, the day Eisenhower briefed his senior commanders in London, the Germans produced a map indicating where they believed the Allied divisions were based. It confirmed that they'd accepted the results of the Allies' deception work from start to finish.

SUPREME HEADQUARTERS
ALLIED EXPEDITIONARY FORCE

Soldiers, Sailors and Airmen of the Allied Expeditionary Force!

You are about to embark upon the Great Crusade, toward which we have striven these many months. The eyes of the world are upon you. The hopes and prayers of liberty-loving people everywhere march with you. In company with our brave Allies and brothers-in-arms on other Fronts, you will bring about the destruction of the German war machine, the elimination of Nazi tyranny over the oppressed peoples of Europe, and security for ourselves in a free world.

Your task will not be an easy one. Your enemy is well trained, well equipped and battle-hardened. He will fight savagely.

But this is the year 1944! Much has happened since the Nazi triumphs of 1940-41. The United Nations have inflicted upon the Germans great defeats, in open battle, man-to-man. Our air offensive has seriously reduced their strength in the air and their capacity to wage war on the ground. Our Home Fronts have given us an overwhelming superiority in weapons and munitions of war, and placed at our disposal great reserves of trained fighting men. The tide has turned! The free men of the world are marching together to Victory!

I have full confidence in your courage, devotion to duty and skill in battle. We will accept nothing less than full Victory!

Good Luck! And let us all beseech the blessing of Almighty God upon this great and noble undertaking.

Dwight D. Eisenhower

CHAPTER FIVE

THE FINAL WEEKEND

By June 1944, after months of frantic preparations, Operation Overlord was finally due to take place. On Monday 5 June the Allies would have to accomplish one of the most significant achievements of the war: sending 156,000 troops to the same place at the same time and in secret. At the end of May hundreds of units were driven to embarkation camps in a move equivalent to relocating the entire population of York and 20,000 vehicles up to 50 miles within five days.

The men of the King's Shropshire Light Infantry were sent south from their sausage camp near Haywards Heath to an embarkation area near Glyndebourne. Private Bob Littlar was feeling confident. His common sense and natural ability had not gone unnoticed, and at Glyndebourne he was promoted to corporal. The KSLI were scheduled to cross the Channel on three large landing-craft, and in early June Littlar and the rest of the men were driven the short distance to the port of Newhaven.

Ike's Order of the Day, issued to all Allied troops

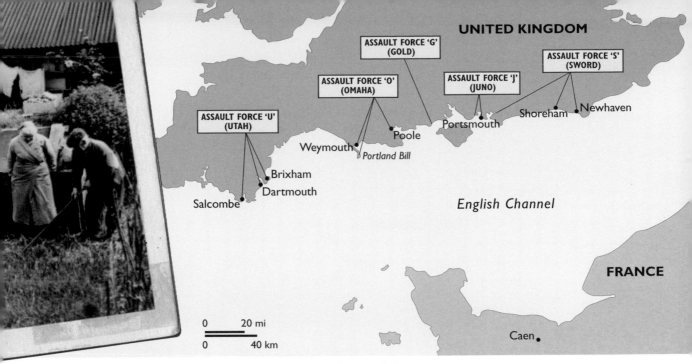

Above right: Map of departure areas used by the five invasion assault forces

Above left: Life carries on as normal as a military convoy snakes its way through Southampton

Left: Map of embarkation camps near Weymouth

Friday 2 June: Down to the dockside

Across southern England vast military convoys were snaking their way from the embarkation camps towards Plymouth, Torquay and Exmouth, Weymouth, Bournemouth and Portsmouth, Southampton, Southsea and Eastbourne. In every port special vehicle slipways – or 'hards' – had been built, piers had been converted into ammunition dumps and above the hundreds of landing-craft silver barrage balloons were buffeted by the breeze.

As the men boarded the boats, they were handed a copy of Eisenhower's Order of the Day, which reminded them that after the 'Great Crusade' the Allies 'will accept nothing less than full victory'. Meanwhile, the naval crews waited for the supreme commander's order that would send them out into open water towards the gathering convoys. At the end of May, Eisenhower had moved down from Bushy Park to

his advance command post. This was a collection of tents and trailers hidden in woods a mile south of Overlord's naval HQ at Southwick House, near Portsmouth. Once Ike gave the word, the armies that would launch the long-awaited invasion would finally begin the 100-mile voyage to Normandy.

As the troops made their way towards the ports, some of the war correspondents who'd be joining them were driven in great secrecy to Wentworth Golf Club, west of London. There they were assigned to their units, and Reuters man Doon Campbell was overjoyed to be told, 'Campbell, commandos, D-Day'. Not all the reporters were so lucky; some wouldn't be going to France for a week. When one complained at missing 'the biggest story since the Crucifixion', an officer replied, 'Yes, but they managed very well with just four correspondents.'

The following day Campbell was driven to a

Overleaf: LCTs and other landing-craft in Southampton

Commandos in training

camp near Southampton, which was occupied by Number 1 Special Service Brigade, commanded by the colourful figure of Lord Lovat. A highly regarded leader, Lovat had taken part in the ill-fated Dieppe raid of 1942. Campbell later wrote that he'd found himself surrounded by men in 'superb shape doing Tarzan acts from the trees'. Trying to suppress feelings of self-consciousness about his artificial arm, he found himself a bunk in the padre's tent.

Life photographer Robert Capa travelled to Weymouth, where he joined the men of the US 1st Infantry Division who were preparing to land on Omaha Beach. Further west, the soldiers of the Utah assault force were boarding their ships, and for many this moment must have rekindled memories of the trauma of Exercise Tiger. That night some units had been decimated and had

since been withdrawn from Overlord. The 3206th Quartermaster Service Company had lost 80 per cent of its men, including Jay Cain. The survivors wouldn't be going to Normandy.

But Jay's twin brother, Corporal Jean Cain, couldn't be spared. Trying to focus on his job, Jean boarded a landing ship, as anxious as any about what lay in store. Eddie McCann, the 15-year-old coxswain who'd pulled 45 survivors from the water during Exercise Tiger, would be sailing in Jean's convoy. Moored off Plymouth, the crew of McCann's ship, LST 515, were once again preparing to take troops on board.

On the evening of 1 June the outside world was given the first hint that the invasion was imminent. At 9.30 p.m. the BBC's French service transmitted coded messages to the Resistance. These included the sentence 'The time of the fight will

come', which caused great excitement among the volunteers. After hearing this on his illegal radio, André Heintz in Caen sent coded postcards to Resistance members hiding in Brittany, urging them to come home. He knew that the next message broadcast by the BBC would indicate that the liberation they'd long been waiting for was finally at hand.

Saturday 3 June: The gathering storm

At RAF Broadwell in Oxfordshire the men of the 9th Parachute Battalion were beginning their last-minute preparations. Having been accused earlier of compromising security, Lieutenant Alan Jefferson was thankful he'd not been pulled from the mission. By Saturday 3 June he had other concerns. His engagement to the ballerina Lisa Grogan had been announced in

the *Daily Telegraph* that morning and he'd found himself the butt of many jokes. Normally there would have been toasts in the bar, but a pre-operation alcohol ban was already in force.

Later that day the soldiers were issued their parachutes, which for some was a procedure accompanied by superstition and ritual. Some serial numbers were considered to be bad omens, and no parachute was ever acceptable if its number ended in 00. As Jefferson later wrote, 00 was 'too final'. For troops taking part in a daring night attack, luck had a hand in everything, not least the weather.

April and May had been largely warm and sunny, but things were about to change. Many naval bases regularly sent weather information to the Admiralty in London. In Dunstable analysts secretly monitored German weather reports,

and in southwest London US Army Air Force experts assembled their own charts. Every day all three centres updated Eisenhower's senior meteorologist, RAF Group Captain James Stagg, who was based at Southwick House. But at the start of June, as the outlook deteriorated, none of the experts could be certain about the weather beyond 48 hours ahead. Opinions clashed and Stagg found it difficult to prepare an accurate forecast.

High winds and rain seemed to be approaching. As Stagg anxiously waited for the latest update on the afternoon of the 3rd, he remembered a light-hearted comment from Lieutenant General Morgan, who'd warned: 'We'll string you up from the nearest lamppost if you don't read the omens right.' By 5 p.m. Stagg was aware he'd have to address the commanders' regular evening briefing and tell Eisenhower that bad weather threatened to disrupt the operation. There was no escaping the image conjured up by Morgan's joke.

Rommel's gamble

German forecasters based in France had also seen that bad weather was coming, and Rommel decided there could be no invasion as long as the Allies' vulnerable landing-craft were at risk from the elements. This gave him an opportunity to tackle the problem that concerned him most – the position of the tank divisions. Exploiting the poor weather, Rommel decided to drive to Germany. Only by leaving his HQ in order to discuss the matter with Hitler would he be able to increase the number of units under his command.

That Saturday morning Rommel set off on the long drive home, via Paris. Meanwhile, his senior officers, also aware of the weather forecast, prepared to take part in an invasion training exercise in Rennes. With no indication that an attack was more likely this weekend than any other, the commanders of the German forces in Normandy made arrangements that would keep them away from their posts on the morning of 5 June. Eisenhower couldn't have asked for more.

Among the Germans' most reliable sources of information in London was Arabel – the Allies' top double agent, Garbo. At 8.20 p.m., as thousands of troops waited to sail for France, Garbo now sent the apparently harmless message suggesting that from this point onwards the Germans should be monitoring their radio all night to hear his latest reports instead of simply listening at prearranged times.

Rommel felt he had a good grasp of the Allies' intentions. He knew the weather conditions needed to launch an invasion, and even believed he had a rough idea where it would come: Calais. But on Saturday 3 June he was distracted. Once he reached Germany, he aimed to tackle the ongoing panzers row – and celebrate his wife's 50th birthday, which was on 6 June. As a result, while preparations for the attack were gathering pace in England, the key German commander responsible for defence in the west was in Paris buying women's shoes and other birthday gifts.

Waiting for Ike

On the evening of the 3rd the Allied soldiers who were to lead the operation were crammed aboard thousands of ships and landing-craft, waiting for their final instructions. Inland, the reinforcement units that were due to sail after D-Day were expecting to move forward to the embarkation areas, while in barracks across Britain the troops who'd be sent to France in the weeks to come were preparing to drive south. The Second Front was less than 48 hours away, and throughout the country more than 2 million people were ready to play their part.

After 16 months of preparation, the combined military machine of Britain, the United States and Canada was ready to operate at maximum capacity. The presence of military personnel from France, Poland, Norway, Belgium, Holland, Australia, New Zealand and South Africa added to the impression that Britain had become one enormous armed camp. In Normandy the Resistance was ready to help at a moment's notice, and with the German commanders distracted, all that remained was for Eisenhower to give the order.

As Ike took his seat in the library of Southwick House at 9.15 p.m. on the evening of the 3rd, his chief weather forecaster was checking his notes. James Stagg was worried. After the latest update, it was now certain that high winds on the night of the 4th would mean that any attack launched on the morning of the 5th would be severely hampered by the weather. After hearing the forecast, Ike – in his lonely position of command – was left with no choice. He asked for the opinions of Montgomery, Ramsay and Leigh-Mallory before provisionally ordering the operation to be delayed for 24 hours.

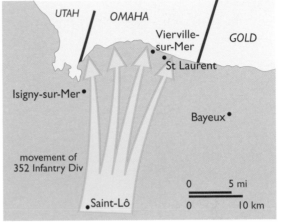

Map showing the German 352nd Infantry Division's advance to the coast

Sunday 4 June: Doubts and delay

At 3.30 a.m. the next morning, Eisenhower drove back to Southwick House from his camp in the woods, and 45 minutes later he reconfirmed his decision to delay. Overnight, vessels that had sailed from northern ports ahead of joining their assault convoys were sent back to refuel, and minesweepers that had already begun to clear safe lanes across the Channel were recalled. Meanwhile, senior officers aboard US command ships had been given the latest intelligence on the German defences.

Most of the German troops on the coast were not regarded as a serious threat – unlike the better-equipped soldiers further inland, such as the 352nd Infantry Division based at St Lô. But the US officers were warned that the 352nd had moved towards the area of Vierville and St Laurent-sur-Mer. To the Allies this was Omaha

Anxious GIs, laden with kit, board a landing-craft

91

Southwick House: the nerve centre of D-Day

Throughout the spring of 1944 General Eisenhower worked at SHAEF HQ in Bushy Park, southwest London. But the site was too far from the action to serve as his HQ on D-Day. It was decided that in the days before the launch of Operation Overlord the supreme commander would move nearer to Admiral Ramsay's naval HQ at Southwick House, north of Portsmouth.

Requisitioned from the Thistlethwayte family in 1941, the building initially housed the Royal Naval School of Navigation, but was taken over by the Allied naval commander-in-chief in 1944. Plotting rooms and training facilities were created, and temporary accommodation huts, workshops and other buildings were constructed in the extensive grounds.

General Montgomery's staff ran the 21st Army Group from tents hidden among trees to the north of the house, and a site was cleared for General Eisenhower and his officers in woods to the south. Ike's camp, code-named 'Sharpener', lay a mile from the main building and included the general's armoured caravans and office tents. Kay Summersby drove Eisenhower up to the house in his Cadillac, and it was in the building's library that he made the historic decision to launch D-Day.

The library was near the map-room, which was the hub of Southwick. The 40 or 50 people who worked in the room included Wrens who plotted the positions of convoys on a huge table. The ships' progress was mapped using chinagraph pencils on Perspex and the plots were frequently updated based on information constantly supplied by radar stations along the coasts.

One wall was devoted to a map of the whole of southern Britain, the Channel and Normandy. This was constructed by a firm that had been ordered to make a map covering the entire European coastline from Norway to Spain. The two workmen who delivered it were told to erect only the Normandy section and were then held at Southwick until D-Day.

King George VI (far left) inspects a naval command room

Beach. It was decided it was too late to pass this news on to the front-line troops, and none of the hundreds of GIs that photographer Robert Capa followed on to the USS *Samuel Chase* troop-ship was warned of the new threat.

In Newhaven, the KSLI had been waiting aboard their landing-craft since the 3rd. On Sunday the 4th they were given the option of returning to shore, where Corporal Littlar and the rest of his platoon were given a splendid Sunday roast. Littlar

may have taken the delay in his stride, but for those men who were already struggling to overcome their anxiety, the postponement proved too much. A soldier on Littlar's boat placed his hand over the barrel of his gun and pulled the trigger. He wasn't the only one.

After the weather, Eisenhower's biggest worry was security, and at no point did these issues give him more concern than on the afternoon of 4 June. The delay increased the chance of an enemy

Overleaf: Allied troops were crammed into landing-craft and barges, which ferried them to troop-ships

agent hearing about the imminent assault. For the Allies, losing the priceless advantage of surprise would give the Germans essential time to bring their panzer divisions from Calais to Normandy.

By June the secret agent Garbo had spent months persuading the Germans that Calais was the Allies' true target. Having urged Madrid to listen out for him all night, he now prepared his D-Day coup de grâce. He was to send a message at 3 a.m. on the morning of the invasion, warning the Germans that troops had embarked, and now he and his case officer, Tomás Harris, used the delay to prepare for the work ahead.

The point of no return

Before leaving Paris for Germany, Rommel had discussed his frustrations with his commander-in-chief, Field Marshal Gerd von Rundstedt. In addition to the panzers row, he still felt the defences along the beaches weren't as strong as they could be. After visiting Corporal Franz Gockel's machine-gun position on Omaha, he'd warned, 'If they come, they'll come here'. The comment had disrupted the betting among Gockel and his comrades on where the Allies would land, and later on so did the worsening weather.

The Germans had access to weather data from across Europe, but conditions in the Channel are shaped by winds from the west. By mid-1944 the Atlantic was largely dominated by the Allies. Their weather ships were able to supply a regular stream of information, and by midday on Sunday the 4th Stagg was told something that Rommel's staff had no way of knowing. The gale blowing in from the west would pass over by the afternoon of the 5th. Monday night and Tuesday morning would be relatively calm.

Throughout Sunday, troops from Falmouth to Portsmouth attended religious services. Reuters correspondent Doon Campbell had got to know the commandos' padre, but he watched in discomfort as the chaplain warned the troops to expect grisly wounds. 'It's God's business,' the padre said, 'and if it wasn't, I wouldn't touch it with a bargepole'. The mood of the congregation was 'awful', Campbell later wrote. Lord Lovat interrupted the service and finished the sermon himself, later telling the padre that he'd damaged the men's morale. The following day Campbell was returning to his tent when he heard a shot ring out. Horrified at what he'd done, the padre had killed himself.

On the Sunday afternoon Churchill toured the war-room at Southwick House accompanied by General de Gaulle, who'd agreed to broadcast to the French people once the invasion had begun. For Ike their presence was a distraction, and he wasn't sorry when they both set off for London. As driving rain lashed the ornate façade of Southwick House, Eisenhower was left alone with his thoughts. At this vulnerable moment only one person could give him the comfort he needed: Stagg, his weather forecaster.

At 9.30 p.m. Stagg arrived to address Ike and the senior commanders, who were again gathered in the library. This time he brought good news. The rain would clear and behind it there would be a period of calm weather. But this wouldn't be perfect: heavy cloud might hamper the Allies' bombers, and unsettled conditions would soon return. Eisenhower again asked his commanders for their opinions, and this time the consensus was to give the order to launch. At 9.45 p.m. Ike simply

D-Day's time bomb

During the Second World War the first day of any major attack by the Allies was simply called 'd-day', the 'd' standing for nothing other than 'day'. (Similarly, 'h-hour' was used to denote the hour of attack.) In this way the day could easily be referred to in plans and telephone calls without the actual date being revealed. In 1944 British and US naval experts, meteorologists, air force officers and army amphibious-warfare specialists worked for weeks to pinpoint the ideal day to launch the invasion of Europe. Originally D-Day was to be 1 May. Eisenhower pushed it back to 1 June to give himself more time to find extra resources, and then left it to the experts to identify the exact date.

The army needed a rising tide shortly after dawn, the air force and airborne divisions wanted clear moonlight, and the navies required slight winds and stable seas. These conditions were only likely to coincide on a relatively small number of days, and the first suitable date after 1 June was 5 June. The 6th was also acceptable, and so was the 7th, but by the 8th the tide would rise so late in the morning that the Germans would have three or four hours to recover after the overnight bombing raids.

Eisenhower was under immense pressure to give the go-ahead as soon as he could. It was known that the Germans were ready to launch their V-1 flying-bombs (the first fell on London just six days after D-Day), and there was no guarantee that the weather would be calm during the next set of suitable days, which fell between 17 and 21 June. Furthermore, Ike knew that using these dates would mean having to accept a new set of difficulties.

If the troops were briefed and ready to go on the 5th, but then delayed until mid-June, 156,000 men would know the secrets of D-Day for two weeks longer than planned. They could not stay aboard their boats for this length of time and would have to be brought ashore. It would be an immense security risk. (In the event, had the invasion been launched in the early hours of 19 June, it would have been devastated by the worst weather to sweep through the Channel in 20 years.) On the evening of 4 June, as Eisenhower considered the options, he knew the fate of millions of people lay in his hands.

said, 'OK, let's go,' and from this point there was no turning back. The invasion was under way.

Monday 5 June: Departure

At 4.30 a.m. on Monday morning Eisenhower received the latest weather report before reconfirming his decision to launch. True to Stagg's word, as the day wore on the rain eased off and the wind began to drop. Monday 5 June had long been scheduled as D-Day, and all preparations had been completed by the 4th. For Eisenhower there was little to do, but for Admiral Ramsay, the commander of the Allies' naval forces, the 5th was a day of

intense activity. Orders were given to the fleet, and the convoys waiting off the coasts began to form up into five assault forces, ahead of the 17-hour passage to Normandy.

The KSLI put to sea at 9.30 a.m. As their landing-craft slipped out of Newhaven, some of the 18-year-old Shropshire lads looked back at the port, uncertain whether they'd see England again. Robert Capa's troop-ship was preparing to sail from Weymouth, Eddie McCann's landing-ship was en route from Plymouth, and the 22 boats carrying Lord Lovat's commandos, accompanied by Doon Campbell, were due

Outside Ike's office tent, 4 June. Kay sits next to Churchill. Ike stands behind them; the strain on his face is evident.

Normandy within 24 hours, Rommel was relaxing at home with his wife and son. He was still awaiting an appointment with Hitler, having left his HQ in the hands of his chief of staff, Lieutenant General Speidel.

That night Speidel was throwing a party. His commitment to Hitler had evaporated, and he enjoyed the company of friends whose views were similar to his own. Seen together, the guests would have been regarded with some suspicion by the Gestapo, and maybe even by Rommel himself.

Unknown to all of them, as they sat down to dinner the BBC's latest coded messages were calling the French Resistance into action. It was announced that 'The dice are on the carpet' and 'It is hot in Suez'. Listening in Caen, André Heintz knew these words were secret orders for railway lines and telegraph wires to be cut.

At Southwick House, Eisenhower had been told that General de Gaulle was now refusing to make his essential D-Day radio broadcast. Frustrated with the demands of politicians, Ike left his command post at 6 p.m. to meet the paratroopers of the US 101st Airborne Division. At RAF Broadwell the men of the British 9th Parachute Battalion had climbed into their bulky combat suits, laden with equipment. While mechanics warmed the engines of the Dakota transport aircraft and WAAFs collected the latest weather information, the skies began to darken and an infectious tension spread among the troops. This time, there'd be no delay. D-Day was finally about to begin.

to leave Southampton. The sea was choppy and the troops knew that an order delaying the operation again was still possible. None came.

On the morning of the 5th Eisenhower, accompanied by his assistant Kay Summersby, watched as British troops boarded landing-craft at Portsmouth. 'There are times,' he told her, 'when you have to put everything you are on the line. This is one of them.' After lunch he spoke to the press, who were forbidden to repeat anything until the soldiers had landed.

In Germany, while Ike was revealing the top-secret plan to send thousands of troops to

CHAPTER SIX

COUNTDOWN TO H-HOUR
5 JUNE 11 P.M. – D-DAY 5 A.M.

On the evening of Monday 5 June many of the men of the US 101st Airborne Division had given themselves Mohican haircuts and daubed their faces with warpaint. When Eisenhower saw them during his tour of four of their airbases in Berkshire he commented: 'They might not scare the Germans, but they certainly scare me.' The paratroopers whistled and shouted as word spread that Ike had come to visit them, and they quickly gathered round their supreme commander and his staff, including Kay Summersby.

The presence of the supreme commander was always a huge attraction, but a lieutenant in the division's 502nd Parachute Infantry Regiment later admitted: 'We were more interested in Ike's driver.' Eisenhower walked from plane to plane, shaking hands with the men and asking where

Ike gives last-minute instructions to US paratroopers at Greenham Common, Berkshire

British paratroopers board a Halifax on the eve of D-Day

they were from. He had a 'wonderfully friendly, man-to-man way, which was one of the strengths of his personality', the divisional commander subsequently wrote, suggesting that it had been a relaxed experience. But Ike later told Kay that it was very hard to look a man in the eye when you fear you might be sending him to his death.

Monday 5 June, 11 p.m: 80 lb of kit and a parachute

While the Americans chatted to the supreme commander, less than 15 miles away the men of the 9th Battalion, the Parachute Regiment, were preparing to clamber into their aircraft at RAF Broadwell. Their target, the Merville Battery, was one of the Allies' most significant objectives in

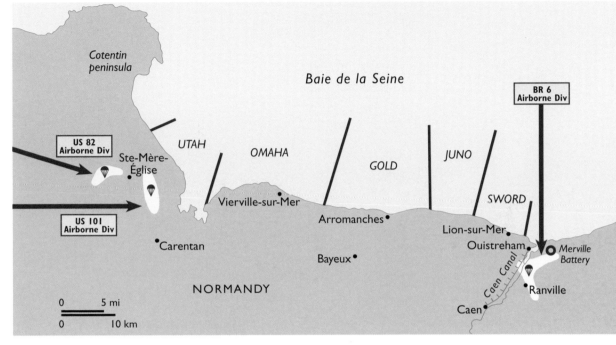

Map showing the D-Day landing zones of the Allied airborne divisions

the first hours of D-Day. If the site's four powerful guns were still intact by dawn, the troops landing on Sword Beach would be dangerously exposed. Lieutenant Alan Jefferson was making sure his 30 soldiers were helping each other with their kit. Each man was carrying up to 80 lb of supplies, and without help from someone else, it was physically impossible to check everything was properly fastened – not least the parachute.

Private Sid Capon was carrying so much kit that he was finding it difficult to walk. Stuffed into his pockets and webbing were a Sten gun, magazines, Mills bombs, phosphorus grenades, ration pack, entrenching tool, message pad, mess tin, wash kit, money, two secret escape compasses, field dressings and his maroon beret. Capon and the rest of Jefferson's platoon hauled

each other into their waiting aircraft just before 11 p.m. Again Capon was struck by the thought that although they'd be plunging into the unknown, at least he and his mates would be together.

As Dakota transport aircraft laden with paratroopers began to take off at airfields across southern England, the dinner party being held by Rommel's chief of staff at La Roche-Guyon was suddenly interrupted. Intelligence officers from the 15th Army in eastern Normandy had decoded one of the BBC messages intended for the French Resistance. They believed the invasion was due to start within hours. But Speidel and his staff had been given so many false reports of an imminent attack in recent weeks that the warnings had started to almost go unnoticed. Disregarding the message, he and his guests returned to their conversation.

Above: US Dakotas preparing to take off for France
Right: Barrage balloons flutter above the invasion fleet as it crosses the Channel at night

But this time the warning was accurate. Fifty miles off the coast of Normandy, 255 minesweepers were shepherding more than 5500 Allied ships through German minefields. On board one of the nine LCIs (landing-craft, infantry) ferrying the British 3rd Infantry Division's 185 Infantry Brigade, Captain John Eaves was clutching a large manilla envelope. As the intelligence officer for the 2nd Battalion of the King's Shropshire Light Infantry, he had known since May where the assault would be. But code-names had been used on the maps previously issued to the rest of the men; their objective, Caen, for example, had been identified only as 'Poland'.

Other than Eaves and his commanding officer, very few men in the battalion knew what the target actually was. But now Eaves ripped open the envelope and passed correctly labelled maps to the officers and senior NCOs. It didn't take long before 18-year-old Corporal Bob Littlar and Private Bill Farmer found out where they were heading. Not that it made much impact – Caen meant little to either of them.

Aboard the USS *Samuel Chase*, photographer Robert Capa was playing poker with other correspondents. With them were a couple of officers from the US 1st Infantry Division's 16th Regiment, with whom Capa was due to land on Omaha Beach. Suddenly the ship's loud hailer ordered the assault troops to begin their preparations, and the game was quickly abandoned.

Horsa gliders near Pegasus Bridge (bottom left)

D-Day, 12 a.m: Airborne divisions lead the way

Above the ships, waves of Dakotas, many towing Horsa gliders, roared towards the distant French coast. Flying as low as 500 ft, aircraft carrying the US 82nd and 101st Airborne Divisions were heading for drop zones to the south of the Cotentin peninsula. Away to their left, British and Canadian paratroopers were being flown to their own landing grounds east of the river Orne.

Ahead of them, the men of the Oxfordshire and Buckinghamshire Light Infantry had already crashed to earth in six gliders at 12.20 a.m. D Company had seized both the bridge over the river Orne and Pegasus Bridge over the Caen Canal, becoming the first Allied soldiers to go

into action in occupied France on D-Day. In a move aimed at preventing German tanks being brought west from Calais, they'd captured the bridges within 15 minutes, and their success has since come to be regarded as one of the most memorable moments in recent British military history.

After a 90-minute flight, the troops of the Parachute Regiment's 9th Battalion jumped at 12.50 a.m. Lieutenant Colonel Otway threw himself out of his unit's lead aircraft, and a minute later his parachute ripped open with a reassuring tug. He was shot at from the ground, and as he landed, he swung into the side of a building. His batman smashed into a nearby greenhouse, but both men survived and made their way to the rendezvous.

While the paratroopers were beginning to assemble, on the other side of the Channel Eisenhower was in a gloomy mood. At 1.15 a.m. he and Kay drove back along moonlit roads to his camp in the woods outside Southwick House. As they waited in an armoured caravan, Ike asked an aide to bring the latest report from the fleet. The aide took a long while to come back, and Eisenhower feared the worst. When he returned with nothing more than a lengthy weather report, Ike was left anxiously wondering when the first update from France would come through. Kay massaged his shoulders and tried to find the right words. He asked her what she was thinking about and she suggested he try and sleep.

1 a.m: Taken by surprise

At La Roche-Guyon, Speidel's remaining guests were starting to leave when vague reports of enemy action began to come in. From 1.30 a.m., warnings of enemy paratroopers were received from General Marcks' 84th Corps at St Lô, the 7th Army at Le Mans and the 716th Infantry Division in Caen. The news was passed to the commander of the German armies in France, Field Marshal von Rundstedt. When his chief of staff, General Blumentritt, heard that the BBC had earlier broadcast a warning of the assault, he asked: 'What kind of general would announce a forthcoming invasion over the radio?' Normandy was clearly under attack, but few German officers believed the threat was significant.

At 1.30 a.m. Lieutenant Colonel Otway reached the rendezvous, a mile east of the Merville Battery, and was met by one of his officers who reported that the drop had been 'bloody chaos'. Later it emerged that so many planes had twisted and weaved to avoid anti-aircraft fire that many men had been carried beyond the drop zone before they'd jumped. Half an hour later just 120 para-troopers out of the 650 soldiers in the battalion had made the rendezvous. Otway had one Vickers machine-gun, but was missing his mortars, medics, anti-tank guns, sappers, mine detectors, wireless sets, explosives and 80 per cent of his men.

As small groups of paratroopers, including Private Sid Capon and Lieutenants Mike Dowling and Alan Jefferson, arrived, Otway knew he would soon have to make one of the toughest decisions of his military career. At 2.30 a.m. he announced that he would wait an extra 15 minutes, and during this time another 30 men turned up. But with so few soldiers, should or shouldn't he attack the battery?

To the French Resistance, the waves of low-flying Dakotas came as no surprise. André Heintz, at home in Caen, was watching the stream of aircraft. Having heard the secret warnings of an imminent invasion broadcast by the BBC, he knew that liberation could be just hours away. André's house was in the same street as the headquarters of the commanding officer of the 716th Infantry Division, so he decided to keep watch on the building.

Inside, Lieutenant General Wilhelm Richter was taking calls from his various divisional outposts dotted around the countryside. Junior officers were sending reports of paratroopers, and among them the commander of the Merville Battery, Lieutenant Raimund Steiner, was passing

on what little he knew. Steiner, an Austrian, was seen by the divisional staff as a foreigner, and a lowly one at that. His warning was hurriedly noted and added to the pile of others.

3 a.m: Duping the Germans
At 2.15 a.m. the chief of staff of the 7th Army told Speidel that he feared the parachute drops amounted to a major operation. But Speidel insisted they were no more than local actions. He was certain that the main thrust of the attack would come in the next few days or weeks, and believed Calais lay at the centre of the Allies' plans. It did. Lieutenant General Morgan's staff had spent almost as much time in developing their deception plan based on Calais as they had on the real thing.

At 3 a.m., in the quiet north London suburb of Hendon, Garbo and his MI5 case officer, Tomás Harris, were watching their vital warning being sent to Madrid by MI5 radio operator Charles Haines. It revealed that the men of the 3rd Infantry Canadian Division were about to embark on ships, suggesting that they would imminently land in France. This was true – the unit was due to seize Juno Beach at 7.45 a.m.

In the time available there was little the Germans could do to prevent the Canadians' attack. However, the truth of the message and the early time that it was sent would potentially raise Garbo's profile to the highest level – as long as it was heard by the Germans. But there was no response from Madrid. Had the Germans finally stopped believing the messages? Haines tried again.

As Garbo's message was being sent, the tank crews of the 21st Panzer Division were warming their engines. The only armoured unit within striking distance of the Normandy coast on 6 June, the formation had first been alerted at 2 a.m. Corporal Werner Kortenhaus, a radio operator in one of the division's 127 Panzer Mk IVs, was awaiting orders, but none came, and it was not clear what the divisional commander, Major-General Edgar Feuchtinger, was planning. In fact, for much of the night few people in the division even knew where Feuchtinger was, and it has since been suggested that he was with his mistress in Paris.

3 a.m: Countdown to attack

At 2.50 a.m. Otway, with only 150 men and very little specialist equipment, decided that the paratroopers' attack on the Merville Battery must go ahead. A seven-man advance party had already set off on a reconnaissance mission, narrowly missing an RAF bombing raid on the way. The bombs had been aimed at the battery, but they'd fallen wide, landing harmlessly in fields 1000 yards away. The advance party reached the target by 3.30 a.m. and, lacking the correct kit, were forced to clear a path through the minefield using only their hands.

Although the US paratroop drops south of the Cotentin peninsula and the British and Canadian drops east of the Orne had been widely reported, German defensive operations were still sporadic and uncoordinated. Rommel's Army Group B was without its talented commander, and had failed to lead or support a swift and powerful response. Whether his reasons were military, political or both, Speidel did not take energetic command of the situation. At around 3.30 a.m. the German Navy realized that the army had underestimated the scale of the attack. Coastal radar stations were receiving signals of an approaching fleet bigger

than anything that had been imagined.

On board the USS *Samuel Chase*, Robert Capa had eaten an early breakfast, and by 3.45 a.m. he was making his final preparations. He would soon be boarding an LCVP landing-craft that would carry him the last 15 miles to Omaha Beach.

On the slopes behind the beach, 18-year-old machine-gunner Corporal Franz Gockel stood shivering in a concrete bunker. It was cold and damp at the best of times, and on this June night Gockel had been told that enemy ships were approaching. Now, staring out to sea, he was just beginning to spot haunting, grey shapes silently looming out of the mist. In the Channel, Robert Capa was struggling to climb into a flat-bottomed landing-craft as it rolled and pitched in 5-ft waves.

Merville: The plan of attack

The Merville Battery was surrounded by a series of strong defences. The compound containing the four huge casemates was protected by an anti-tank ditch up to 10 ft deep, and beyond this two belts of barbed wire surrounded the whole site. Between the two lines of wire lay a minefield.

A total of around 1000 bombs had been dropped on the compound over many nights, and by D-Day the cratered landscape resembled the surface of the moon. The garrison was believed to be 160-strong, and these men would be manning the battery's 15-odd machine-gun nests.

Otway's plan of attack went as follows:

0020: Pathfinders of the 22nd Independent Parachute Company land on the drop zone, a mile and a quarter east of the battery and illuminate it for the main battalion. Reconnaissance party and rendezvous parties due to land.

0030: RAF to bomb battery. Reconnaissance party to head directly for the site and prepare to report on success of RAF raid.

0050: 32 aircraft arrive over drop zone, bringing the main body of the battalion.

0235: Battalion due to leave drop zone and head for battery. (Otway personally decides he's prepared to wait until 0250 if things aren't going according to plan.)

0240: Three Horsa gliders take off, carrying men of A Company and specialists.

0410: Battalion to reach 'Firm Base', 500 yards away from the battery.

0425: Star shells to explode, illuminating battery for approaching gliders; paratroopers to begin firing on battery; diversion party to suggest attack is beginning at main gate.

0427: Fire to cease on bugle call (except diversion party).

0430: Gliders due to land; bugle call to signal start of attack; B Company to blow gaps in the inner wire and C Company to attack gun casemates.

0500: Otway to fire flare, signalling success of attack to HMS Arethusa offshore.

0530: Arethusa to open fire, if no signal received from battery; Otway to lead men to next task, seizing village of Le Plein.

At the Merville Battery, Otway had brought his men up to the belt of barbed wire that surrounded the site. It was 4.20 a.m. and he'd started to throw occasional glances at the sky in search of the three gliders he knew would be arriving in the next few minutes. Supported by just a fraction of his men, Otway had been forced to radically rewrite his plan. Lieutenant Mike Dowling's platoon, originally tasked with simply blowing the wire, would now also be joining the actual assault on the guns, and he, Lieutenant Jefferson and the other junior officers, now began to prepare their soldiers for the attack.

4.30 a.m: Assault on the Merville Battery

Jefferson and Dowling were each put in command of one of the four assault groups, one group per gun, comprising a total of 50 men. While a diversion party made as much commotion as possible at the main gate, the groups would launch the attack from the rear of the battery. Jefferson told his soldiers to think of their wives and sweethearts, and to remember that Nazis had to be killed if their families were to be protected. After he'd spoken he waited in the darkness, his body pumping with adrenalin.

At around 4.25 a.m. star shells were to be fired over the target: their piercing glare was intended

to bring in the gliders. But the shells had been lost in the chaotic drop, along with most of the other specialist kit. With time running short, Otway had to launch the assault with what he had. Suddenly, German machine-guns erupted, and on Otway's command the paratroopers shot back, spraying the compound with bursts of automatic fire that ripped through the darkness from all angles.

Two minutes later the men stopped shooting and waited for the gliders, which were due to land any minute. Out of the darkness two box-like Horsa gliders suddenly swept low over the waiting troops, while anti-aircraft shells burst in the air around

them. Without star shells to guide them, one came down 100 yards away, the other disappeared into the distance and the third didn't arrive at all. None crash-landed on the battery as they were supposed to: the Royal Engineers' explosives experts, their kit and the 66 extra paratroopers Otway had been waiting for were all in the wrong place. Again, Otway decided to push on regardless and gave the signal to launch the attack.

Using tube-like Bangalore torpedoes, Dowling's men blew gaps in the wire. Jefferson sprang into the compound and ran towards one of the huge concrete bunkers while firing his Sten gun from the hip. As enemy soldiers shot at

them from all directions, Private Sid Capon and the rest of the assault troops followed closely behind.

5 a.m: Mission accomplished

A mile to the north, the commanding officer of the Merville Battery, Lieutenant Raimund Steiner, was inside a control bunker and could hear the crescendo of firing and screams. Thinking of a way to help, he had an idea that was shocking but something he knew he had to do. He rang his men and warned them that he was going to ask the Houlgate Battery further east to fire its guns at them. He knew that while his soldiers would be safe in their concrete shelters, the shells from the neighbouring position would kill anyone caught in the open. Making a second call, he ordered a barrage on his own command.

Inside the Merville Battery the battle was raging. Machine-gunners fired at the sprinting paratroopers, and a bullet pierced Jefferson's left leg, bringing him to the ground. Private Capon ran on and entered the first gun bunker, yelling at the top of his voice. He opened fire, while behind him other men tried to destroy the gun. At the same time similar things were happening in the other three gun bunkers. The paratroopers didn't find modern German weapons as expected, but

discovered instead smaller Czech guns of First World War vintage. Regardless of their age, they were difficult to destroy without the right kit.

Outside the bunkers, Lieutenant Dowling found Otway and told him the mission had been accomplished. 'Are you sure all the guns are out of action?' asked Otway, and Dowling replied that he would personally go back and examine them. But as he ran shells began to fall, some detonating landmines buried near the casemates. Suddenly the flash of a huge explosion lit up the compound and the blast killed Dowling instantly.

When the attack ended at around 5 a.m. the men retreated, taking with them their injured comrades and 23 prisoners. Of the 150 para-troopers who took part in the assault, half were killed or wounded, but the remainder believed the mission had been a success. Although a signal flare was fired and a carrier pigeon released, the troops had no way of confirming that the messages would get through to HMS *Arethusa* waiting offshore. They escaped south towards the village of Le Plein, aware that a merciless bombardment by the Royal Navy was due to begin at 5.30 a.m.

CHAPTER SEVEN

THE BATTLE FOR THE BEACHES
D-DAY 5 A.M. – 10 A.M.

At around dawn on 6 June Robert Douin, the map-maker, knew something unusual was happening as he looked out of his cell window in Caen prison. He didn't quite know what, but he wasn't alone in hoping an Allied operation was finally about to begin. There had been the usual heavy bombing raids during the night, but this time there were many low-flying planes that hadn't dropped bombs. The guards were disturbed about some order or other, and then came proof that freedom was at hand: the sound of guns.

The Allies' naval guns were immense weapons that lobbed shells, weighing up to a ton, across more than 10 miles of open sea. The tremendous bombardment that erupted off the Normandy coastline at 5.30 a.m. wasn't a random hammering of the defences but a carefully planned part of the whole operation.

Naval guns batter targets on Omaha immediately prior to the landings

Ships repeatedly targeted German bunkers, trying to pick off the enemy strongpoints before the troops reached the shore.

An hour and a half before the bombardment began, photographer Robert Capa had pulled himself into a lurching LCVP landing-craft, its deck slippery with oil and sea water. While the battleships were firing, Capa's boat was one of many circling around them, waiting for the order to head for the beaches. Standing inside the LCVPs, the GIs could see the huge shells screaming overhead.

The troops were struggling to endure seasickness and a numbing blanket of fear. With the reality of battle looming, many of the wet and shivering soldiers were vomiting as their boats were tossed about in 5-ft waves. Some prayed aloud and most were already halfway to exhaustion. They tried to see where they were heading, but grey clouds seemed to slide seamlessly into the churning sea as smoke from the bombardment obscured the formidable defences of Omaha Beach.

In a tent in the grounds of Southwick House a phone was ringing. Air Chief Marshal Sir Trafford Leigh-Mallory wanted to give Eisenhower a glowing but unwittingly misleading report on the night's glider operations. An aide took the note to Ike after 6 a.m., expecting to find him asleep, but the general was sitting up in bed and speaking on the phone to Admiral Ramsay. Soon after Eisenhower got up he dictated a cable to Washington, saying he'd not yet had any news about the progress of the troops. Six hours after

the first shots of D-Day were fired, both the
Allied and German commanders had little confirmation about what was actually happening on
the ground.

6.30 a.m: Devastation on Omaha

Corporal Franz Gockel was in little doubt about
what was going on. After the naval bombardment
and subsequent air raids the timid 18-year-old
machine-gunner had all the evidence he needed
that this was the real thing. Crouching behind
5-ft-thick concrete walls, he'd been badly shaken
but still believed he had a good chance of
surviving all but a direct hit. At 6.30 a.m. Gockel's
gun position overlooking the beach was still
intact, and now, heading directly towards it, were
scores of landing-craft full of GIs.

On the western end of Omaha seasoned Royal
Navy crews landed the inexperienced US 116th
Infantry Regiment. This part of the beach was
defended by the highly capable German 352nd
Infantry Division, which US commanders had
only recently been told was in the area. The 200
GIs of the 116th's Company A landed at 6.30 a.m.
and even had time to line up before advancing
together. But they hadn't got far when the
machine-gun nests embedded in the ridge
behind Omaha opened up. The powerful
weapons fired horizontally along the beach and
the men pinned down on the sand had nowhere
to hide.

The onslaught was devastating and complete.
The scale of destruction on this part of Omaha at
this time of the day was of First World War

proportions: Company A, mostly made up of men from the small Virginia town of Bedford, suffered around 90 per cent casualties. At the eastern end of the beach, where the experienced 16th Regiment was landing, things weren't much easier.

Among the first units to land here was the 16th's E Company, which found itself on a stretch of sand code-named Easy Red. Capa said these were the men he accompanied, though he might actually have landed an hour or so later. As the ramp on his LCVP landing-craft dropped to the water, he immediately began taking pictures: a snatched wide shot of the beach; soldiers ducking behind one of the steel obstacles; a lone GI neck-deep in the water. Capa then plunged into the cold surf before scrambling on

to the beach, where he captured the frantic efforts of men clinging to life, while lying immersed in the terror himself.

On the grassy slopes 400 yards opposite Capa, Gockel had waited until the troops started to come up the beach before firing his machine-gun. Since then, he'd barely lifted his finger from the trigger. He may have been protected by concrete walls, but the teenager was as scared as any of the men in front of him. And all the time more GIs were landing. LCVP coxswain Eddie McCann, the 15-year-old who'd rescued survivors during Exercise Tiger, had been bringing in soldiers since the first minutes of the assault. Screaming for the troops to get off his boat, he knew their lives depended on reinforcements –

and the reinforcements were depending on him. There were precious few landing-craft, and he needed to get back to the troop-ships.

7 a.m: The first German response

South of Caen, the German 21st Panzer Division was just starting to get organized. During the night it had remained on alert, but no orders had been issued. Finally, at around 7 a.m., the divisional commander, Major-General Feuchtinger, returned to his HQ. He sent around 40 of his tanks east of the river Orne towards the positions held by British paratroopers, including Otway's battered battalion. At this point on D-Day 21st Panzer was the only German armoured unit advancing on Allied troops.

Above: Corporal Franz Gockel
Overleaf: One of Capa's first pictures of
Omaha, taken from the ramp of his LCVP

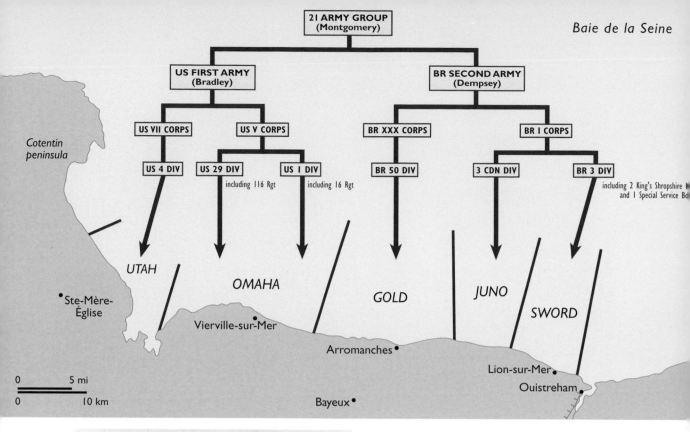

21 ARMY GROUP
(Montgomery)

US FIRST ARMY
(Bradley)

BR SECOND ARMY
(Dempsey)

US VII CORPS

US V CORPS

BR XXX CORPS

BR I CORPS

US 4 DIV

US 29 DIV
including 116 Rgt

US I DIV
including 16 Rgt

BR 50 DIV

3 CDN DIV

BR 3 DIV
including 2 King's Shropshire
and I Special Service Bd

Cotentin
peninsula

UTAH

OMAHA

GOLD

JUNO

SWORD

Ste-Mère-
Église

Vierville-sur-Mer

Arromanches

Lion-sur-Mer

Ouistreham

Bayeux

0   5 mi

0   10 km

Map of Allied assault units and their target areas

Amphibious DUKW vehicle, known as a 'duck'

At home in Herrlingen, southern Germany, Rommel was awaiting an appointment with Hitler to discuss control of the tank divisions in northern France. The phone rang at 6.30 a.m. and thoughts of political arguments vanished when Speidel told Rommel that paratroopers had landed. However Speidel said it was a local action and insisted there was no cause for alarm.

At La Roche-Guyon the first reports were coming in of seaborne soldiers landing to the east of the Cotentin peninsula. By 7.30 a.m. US troops had been fighting on Utah and Omaha for an hour. Of all the five invasion beaches, Utah was the first to be brought under Allied control, and the soldiers landing there suffered the fewest casualties, with 197 men killed or wounded.

The Utah assault force lost nearly four times more troops in training than in battle, and for some, D-Day was almost an insignificance compared to the horrors of Exercise Tiger. Corporal Jean Cain was in action from the start. Driving his amphibious 'duck' truck from a landing-craft offshore, he aimed directly for the beach, dodging exploding German shells.

While Cain was bringing supplies to the troops on Utah, 50 miles to the east hundreds of British and Canadian soldiers had begun landing on Gold, Juno and Sword. Parts of Gold were as undefended as Utah; others were comparable to Omaha. On Juno the Canadians fought hard to overwhelm the German defences, while on Sword the initial

Operation Gambit: D-Day's best-kept secret

The invasion beaches weren't randomly chosen stretches of sand, but carefully selected military objectives that had been thoroughly researched over many months. It was found that some sections of certain beaches were less well defended than others, and the naval commanders knew it was their duty to ensure the assault troops were taken to exactly the right spot.

In an operation involving thousands of soldiers and a fleet of nearly 6000 vessels, precise navigation was essential. If the first boats were off course, they could delay the entire invasion. In late 1943 the admirals turned their minds to finding a way of ensuring this didn't happen.

Their solution was the X-craft, a mini-submarine that would be positioned on the seabed directly opposite the point where the first troops would land. The 50-ft submarine had a hand-picked crew of five, who were trained to work under great pressure in extremely confined conditions. Surfacing an hour or so before the fleet arrived, the sailors would shine a guiding light out to sea towards the approaching boats.

Only two X-craft were available for D-Day, and after the Americans declined the offer of using one it was decided that the vessels would be stationed off Sword and Juno. The crews of X-23, commanded by Lieutenant George Honour, and X-20, under Lieutenant Ken Hudspeth, were sent to Portsmouth in January to train for their top-secret mission, code-named Operation Gambit.

Maintaining radio silence, the subs were towed across the Channel on the night of 2 June and took up their positions before sinking to the seabed. When the sailors received a signal announcing D-Day had been delayed, they prepared to spend another 24 hours under water. At dawn on the morning of the 6th they surfaced in the correct positions and carried out their orders to perfection.

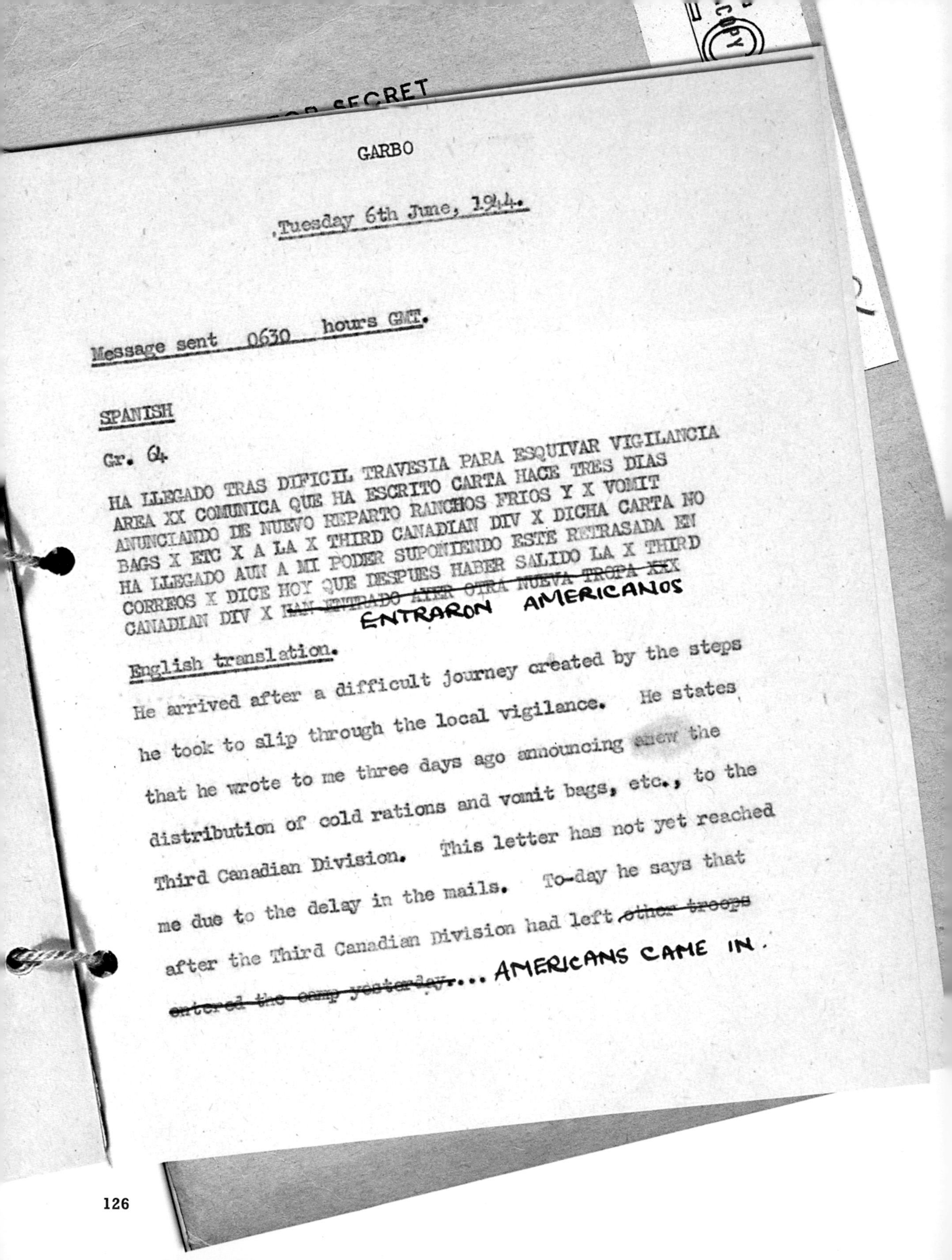

GARBO

Tuesday 6th June, 1944.

Message sent   0630   hours GMT.

SPANISH

Gr. 64

HA LLEGADO TRAS DIFICIL TRAVESIA PARA ESQUIVAR VIGILANCIA
AREA XX COMUNICA QUE HA ESCRITO CARTA HACE TRES DIAS
ANUNCIANDO DE NUEVO REPARTO RANCHOS FRIOS Y X VOMIT
BAGS X ETC X A LA X THIRD CANADIAN DIV X DICHA CARTA NO
HA LLEGADO AUN A MI PODER SUPONIENDO ESTE RETRASADA EN
CORREOS X DICE HOY QUE DESPUES HABER SALIDO LA X THIRD
CANADIAN DIV X ~~HAN ENTRADO AYER OTRA NUEVA TROPA XXX~~
ENTRARON AMERICANOS

English translation.

He arrived after a difficult journey created by the steps

he took to slip through the local vigilance.   He states

that he wrote to me three days ago announcing anew the

distribution of cold rations and vomit bags, etc., to the

Third Canadian Division.   This letter has not yet reached

me due to the delay in the mails.   To-day he says that

after the Third Canadian Division had left ~~other troops~~

~~entered the camp yesterday~~ ... AMERICANS CAME IN.

126

Above: Lord Lovat (to the right of the column of men) wades onto Sword Beach. His piper is in the foreground.

Left: Part of Garbo's message sent after 6 a.m. in which he refers to the fictitious Agent 4

assault had gone relatively well. The troops of the British 3rd Infantry Division had pushed forward and were fighting for the villages immediately behind the beach. By 8 a.m. news of their success had reached the KSLI, who were still aboard their three landing-craft.

Corporal Bob Littlar and Private Bill Farmer had come to know a man with a reputation for getting hold of extra supplies. Private 'Gisser' Owens had won his nickname from frequent requests to 'give us a cigarette' – or whatever else was on offer. Every battalion had its memorable characters, and among the KSLI's was Gisser. Looking out to sea, Owens, Littlar and Farmer saw so many ships that it seemed they could almost walk home without getting their feet wet.

8 a.m: Fighting for the beaches

Vital parts of the operation remained strictly hidden from view. While the assault troops tackled the enemy's front-line defensive positions, the German commanders were being dealt with by the Allies at a higher level. In London Garbo was back at work. His 3 a.m. message, repeated three hours later, reporting that the landings were imminent had gone unnoticed, so at 8 a.m. his radio operator tried again. After a pause, the message was finally acknowledged. The news might have been old, but Garbo's credibility with the Germans still climbed another notch.

The commando unit that Reuters reporter Doon Campbell was accompanying sent its first men on to Sword Beach at 8.30 a.m. Led by Lord Lovat, their mission was to advance south, then cross the river Orne to rendezvous with the 9th Parachute Battalion – Otway's men. As Lovat pushed through the surf, he was accompanied by his personal piper, who was leading the commandos forward to the tune of 'Blue Bonnets'.

It couldn't have been more different from Omaha. The GIs had been ashore for two hours and in that time they'd made little progress. Here and there the odd platoon had reached the slopes beyond the beach, and some troops had even climbed to the top. But the vast majority were still crouching behind the sea wall, pinned down by machine-guns and mortars. Around them lay the debris of a vast military assault. Tanks, bulldozers, boats and bodies lay battered and torn in the rising tide.

Sheltering beside rusting beach obstacles and a burnt-out tank, Robert Capa had managed to take more than 100 pictures. By 8.30 a.m. he'd had enough. Hanging on to the precious films, he waded though the bloody surf and hauled himself on to a departing coastguard LCI . He was lying beside the warmth of its engine when the boat took a direct hit from a German shell, but it stayed afloat and headed out to sea. Above the beach, Gockel was still blazing away at the US soldiers, aware that they were getting closer and closer. He wasn't expecting to stop the invasion, he was simply trying to survive it.

Meanwhile, 40 tanks of the 21st Panzer Division had advanced east of the river Orne in search of the British. As they trundled towards the ground held by the paratroopers, they were directly taken over at 8.45 a.m. by General Marcks, who at that time was probably more aware of the extent of the Allied operation than any other German officer. In the absence of a direct order from Speidel, Marcks – the commander of the 84th Corps – stepped in and ordered the tanks to come back west of the Orne. He was concerned at the British advance from Sword Beach.

9 a.m: Waiting for news

At around 9 a.m. Eisenhower was given the latest naval report. It simply said that all was going to plan and was timed at 6.52 a.m. He congratulated Lieutenant General Morgan for his early work on the invasion proposals, Morgan modestly replying: 'Well, you finished it.' Kay then drove Eisenhower the short distance to Montgomery's HQ. Ike was keen for a radio bulletin to be broadcast announcing the success of the landings, but Montgomery's people wanted to hold back until they had more confirmation. Eventually they were satisfied, and the BBC was given a brief statement.

The news agencies, desperate for more information, were relying on their correspondents and had no way of knowing when they would get the first eye-witness reports.

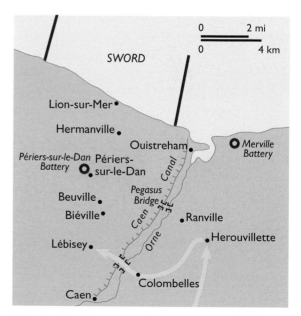

Map showing the movements of the German 21st Panzer Division on the morning of D-Day

At 9.06 a.m. Reuters reporter Doon Campbell was clambering on to Sword Beach. Anxiously trying to hide his false arm from the commandos whose trust he needed to maintain, he made his way to a crater. With tanks clanking past and officers yelling instructions all around him, he began to bash out some copy, until earth from the blasts of mortar shells clogged the typewriter keys. Turning to pen and paper, he tried to assess the bigger picture on the beach and beyond.

Six miles south of Campbell some of the prisoners in Caen prison had been taken from their cells. Earlier they'd sung at the sound of the naval guns, but now an air of fear permeated the stone building. Barking out orders, the German guards lined the men up and checked their names against a list. The prisoners, all Resistance volunteers, were then roughly shoved towards the prison's courtyard.

Locked in his cell, Robert Douin could hear shouting and he wondered what was happening. Then another sound ricocheted around the prison, and Douin listened in utter disbelief. He could hear occasional cries as the terrible clatter of machine-guns echoed again and again around the stark stone walls.

At around 9 a.m., in a mountain retreat in Bavaria, German staff officers were examining an update from one of the army commands. It confirmed earlier reports sent to their small telephone exchange during the night, and

The BBC's John Snagge announced the news of the landings

after reading it, their duty was clear. Certain that an invasion was under way, one of them had to inform Hitler. The German state radio service had broadcast an announcement at 7 a.m. confirming that the Allies had landed in France, but the facts had been toned down and any note of alarm was drowned out by a chorus of approval at the prospect of battle.

In Britain the BBC reported at 9.32 a.m. that Allied ships had begun landing troops on the coast of France early that morning. After the bulletin the BBC broadcast a pre-recording by Eisenhower, urging Resistance forces across the Continent to follow the instructions previously issued to them. Throughout Europe people were waking to the news that the Second Front was finally under way, and everywhere a similar hope was shared: that the end of the war was in sight.

In a flat in London's Upper Wimpole Street John Morris was listening to the radio. For most people the morning's news brought excitement, but Morris knew that for him the announcement meant hours of anxious waiting. As the London picture editor for *Life* magazine, it was his job to get the first photographs of the invasion back to the United States. But until the negatives arrived, there was little he could do.

As Morris absorbed news of the landings, he

Canadian troops, equipped with bicycles, land on Juno Beach at high tide

knew that somewhere in the middle of the battle on the beaches his close friend Robert Capa would be risking his neck. Unlike the soldiers beside him, the photographer had the luxury of being able to escape whenever he wanted to in order to get his films back to London. The question was, when would they arrive? Morris hurriedly left the flat and headed for his office in Soho.

9.30 a.m: Ghosts at Merville

Lieutenant Colonel Otway was exhausted. After leaving the Merville Battery, he led his remaining 75 soldiers southwest towards his next objective, the village of Le Plein. En route he left 22 of his wounded men, including Lieutenant Alan Jefferson, at a farmhouse near the battery, along with two German medical orderlies who'd been captured during the battle. While lying on the floor of the building, Jefferson overheard some of the men talking softly, and for the first time he discovered that his close friend Lieutenant Mike Dowling had been killed. Remembering the dream he and Dowling shared of setting up an orange farm abroad, Jefferson wept at the loss of his friend. He then decided he had to look for his body. At around 9.15 a.m., as the rest of the battalion was taking up position near Le Plein 2 miles away, Jefferson ordered one of the German medics to accompany him back to the site of the dawn attack.

As he approached the rows of barbed wire, Jefferson slowly came to the disturbing realization that he shouldn't be there. He couldn't actually

see any bodies, but no birds were singing, and a pervading sense of death weighed upon him so heavily that he decided to go no further.

At around 10 a.m. Jefferson and the orderly turned round and returned to the farmhouse, leaving behind them an ominous stillness that hung over the whole battery compound.

10 a.m: The race to reach Caen

Certain prisoners the Gestapo deemed too important to be allowed to fall into Allied hands had been earmarked for transfer to Germany should the Allies ever approach Caen. But by 6 June the city's railway system had suffered so much damage that it was impossible to move them by train. Road travel too was out of the

question as petrol was scarce and could not be wasted on transporting prisoners. As far as the Gestapo were concerned, only one option remained. In the small hours of the morning they sent an execution order and an accompanying list of names to the commandant of Caen prison. Men's fate depended on a piece of paper.

By mid-morning, the sound of automatic gunfire had been echoing around the building for what seemed like days. There was no break in the rattle of machine-guns as French Resistance volunteers were systematically killed in the courtyard. Groups of men, deprived of hope but still clinging to dignity, were led into the sunshine six at a time. A man with a wooden leg slipped over in the blood and was shot where he lay.

Caen was the objective of the troops of the British 3rd Infantry Division, and by 10 a.m. they'd been landing on Sword Beach for more than two hours. While soldiers streamed ashore, landing-craft crews out at sea waited to bring in the next wave of men, including the KSLI. If Caen was to be reached by nightfall on D-Day, the Allies would have to land enough troops and vehicles to roll the Germans back by 8 miles. Throughout April and May General Montgomery had been in no doubt that this could be done, but it was too optimistic, and on 6 June his plans quickly began to fall behind schedule.

10 a.m: Chaos on the beaches

On Sword Beach, burnt-out tanks and trucks littered the sand. Barbed wire and wood, sandbags and rifles, clothing, webbing and bodies lay strewn about as boats of all types struggled to land in the right spot at the right time. As men from dozens of different units – infantry, demolition specialists, medics, intelligence teams – waded on to the beach, the overly ambitious landing schedules began to break down. Waiting aboard three large landing-craft a mile out to sea, the KSLI were delayed in coming ashore. The men were ordered below decks and, ever fearful of mines, they could feel the vessel grinding over sandbanks.

Further west the confusion was even worse. Things were moving slowly on Sword, but at least the first wave of troops had already started to sweep inland. On Omaha the death-toll was still relentlessly climbing, and groups of terrified men remained hemmed in beneath the lip of the low sea wall. Waiting aboard a US flagship, the commander of the US First Army, Lieutenant General Bradley, was handed the first report from Omaha shortly before 10 a.m. It said little more than 'obstacles mined, progress slow', but he ordered the message to be sent to Eisenhower.

Small-boat coxswain Eddie McCann was still bringing in troops, 30 at a time. He'd been racing back and forth to the beach for four hours, and he and his crew, who'd been at sea since 4 a.m., were extremely tired. Before they'd left their landing-ship, they'd been given rations by some of the soldiers, and while at sea they tried to swallow hard crackers, Spam and cheese.

Time and again McCann ferried reinforcements out to the beach and brought wounded men back to the fleet.

On the USS *Samuel Chase* troop-ship, a small bag containing rolls of 35mm film lay on a table beside the collapsed figure of an unidentified man. Robert Capa had been helped aboard by the crew of the landing-craft he'd met on Omaha. Once back on the ship, he'd begun to take pictures of the wounded and dying men lying on the crowded decks. Then his head had started to swim, things became confused and he suddenly passed out. He was taken to a bunk and a label was hung around his neck: 'Exhaustion case. No dog tags.' For him the worst was over. Fifty miles away to the east, for the KSLI D-Day was about to begin.

Robert Capa

Born Endre Friedmann in Budapest in 1913, Robert Capa left home at 18 and found a job as a darkroom apprentice with a Berlin picture agency. With the rise of Hitler, Friedmann, who was Jewish, fled to Paris in 1933, and helped by his German-Jewish girlfriend, Gerda Pohorylle, he tried to get established as a freelance photographer.

In the spring of 1936 Endre and Gerda decided to form an association of three people. Gerda acted as sales representative, Endre was a darkroom hired hand, and both were supposedly employed by a rich, famous and imaginary American photographer named Robert Capa. Friedmann took the pictures, Gerda sold them, and credit was given to the non-existent Capa, whose shots went for three times the standard rate.

That summer Friedmann, now openly operating under the name of Capa and accompanied by Gerda, covered the civil war in Spain. He won international acclaim for his remarkable picture of a dying loyalist militiaman. In 1937 Gerda, who'd become a photographer in her own right, was crushed to death by a tank after finding herself caught in a hurried retreat. Grief-stricken, Capa went to China, where he took a series of memorable pictures at the battle of Taierzhuang before later returning to Spain.

When the United States joined the Second World War in 1941, Capa was in the USA and initially found difficulty getting a posting to the front. But in 1942 he was finally sent on an assignment that took him to Britain, North Africa and Sicily, where he witnessed the grim winter campaign of 1943-4. In April 1944, he left Italy for London, and threw himself into card games and partying before sailing from Weymouth ahead of D-Day.

By 6 June Capa had gained an internationally recognized reputation, underlined by articles such as the eight-page spread that appeared in the prestigious British magazine Picture Post in December 1938. It was headlined 'The Greatest War Photographer in the World'.

CHAPTER EIGHT

THE ADVANCE SOUTH
D-DAY 10 A.M. – 4 P.M.

By 10 a.m. the troops of the KSLI had been brought up to the open decks of their boats, which had begun to manoeuvre towards the shore. As artillery shells slammed into the sea, Corporal Littlar gingerly peered over the rail at Sword Beach, which lay shrouded in smoke.

At 10.10 a.m. Littlar, Privates Owens and Farmer, Captain Eaves and Major Peter Steel plunged neck-deep into the heaving surf and, following ropes tied by the navy, fought hard to haul themselves on to the beach. Farmer struggled to keep his Bren gun above his head, knowing it would be useless if it got wet. Either side of the men, the water boiled beneath the artillery fire, while behind them a landing-craft started to sink after taking a direct hit.

Sword Beach on the early morning of D-Day

The soldiers were carrying sandbags stuffed full of extra supplies, which they planned to dump in a vast pile on the beach, ready to be collected by support troops in a day or two. Dodging craters and mortar fire, the KSLI dropped their extra kit and began cautiously to advance a mile inland. They were heading towards their first rendezvous point, the village of Hermanville, which had been secured earlier by the first wave of troops.

Rommel had first heard about the Allies' assault when Speidel alerted him at 6.30 a.m. Anxious to hear the latest developments, he spoke to his chief of staff for a second time at around 10 a.m. The news wasn't good, and the field marshal realized he had to return to his post as quickly as possible. Cancelling his planned meeting with Hitler, Rommel left his home in Herrlingen for the long drive back to France.

By 10 a.m. the outdated Mark IV tanks of the German 21st Panzer Division had already been sent towards the areas held by the British paratroopers. Before Rommel left for France General Marcks, having earlier been given direct control of the unit, had decided that the real threat lay not with the paratroopers east of the river Orne, but with the troops marching south from the beaches. He'd instructed the tanks to cross to the west of the Orne, but his order was slow to get through to the men on the ground.

Finally, at 10.30 a.m., around 40 tanks received an order to cross back to the western side of the

river, which was where they'd originally come from that morning. The nearest bridge, code-named Pegasus by the Allies, had been captured by British airborne troops during the night, and 21st Panzer Division was forced to use the next bridge further south, at Colombelles. Much time had been lost in moving east of the river, and by mid-morning on D-Day none of the division's 127 tanks had yet fired a shot.

10 a.m: Fear and uncertainty

In Caen prison Jacques Collard, aged just 15, had been ordered out of his cell and told to join a line of prisoners. The terrified teenager followed the group of men as they walked downstairs towards the courtyard, where machine-guns were still relentlessly firing. When they approached an open door, a guard caught sight of Jacques and, seeing how young he was, dragged the boy out of the line and sent him back to his cell. On the way Jacques spotted his father coming down the stairs in another group of men and, in an atmosphere charged with emotion, they told each other to take courage.

By 10.30 a.m. the gunfire had stopped. But for the surviving prisoners the silence brought more questions than the shooting, and they furtively tried to swap information. Inside his cell, Robert Douin had no way of knowing that the Gestapo's henchmen had left the prison. After changing out of their bloodstained tunics, they had returned to their HQ in the middle of the city and were preparing to flee south to Falaise.

Across the Channel, few updates were reaching Eisenhower. Hundreds of radio messages had actually been received from the fleet, including Lieutenant General Bradley's report on the situation at Omaha. But so many signals were being filed from the different British and US command ships that naval cypher clerks in England were struggling to keep up. Several messages had yet to be decoded.

After spending time with General Montgomery, Eisenhower left to inspect Admiral Ramsay's war-room at Southwick House. He was told that two ships had been lost, one – the Norwegian destroyer *Svenner* – having been sunk by German torpedo boats. Ramsay's staff also reported that the waves were a little high for some of the smaller craft, and the wind was still strong, but overall things were going to plan. One of Ike's aides noted that all was well with the navy and 'their smiles were wide as any'.

Above: The village of Hermanville-sur-Mer, a mile behind Sword Beach

Left: Admiral Ramsay and General Eisenhower at Southwick House early on D-Day

11 a.m: Opening up the bridgehead

After slowly moving through the countryside beyond the beach, Gisser Owens, Corporal Littlar and Private Farmer reached an apple orchard near the village of Hermanville at around 11 a.m. As they sat down among the trees, they and the rest of the KSLI brewed mugs of tea and waited for their next set of orders. They were slightly behind schedule, but so far all seemed to be going as well as could be expected.

The battalion's intelligence officer, Captain John Eaves, had put away his first set of maps and was examining an envelope containing the details of their main objective: Caen. The troops were exactly where they were supposed to be and were supported by the other two units in their brigade – one battalion from the Royal Norfolk Regiment and another from the Royal Warwick-

shire Regiment. Like the KSLI, both were made up of 600 men and both were regrouping near Hermanville.

As the troops of the US 1st Infantry Division gradually began to push beyond Omaha Beach, news of the Allies' progress was passed to Hitler. After arriving at Klessheim Castle, where he was due to host a Hungarian state visit, he was quickly given the latest battle reports. The Führer gazed at a map of France before declaring in unusually broad Austrian tones: 'So, we're off.'

At noon Churchill addressed the House of Commons, then he and King George VI were driven to watch the assault being mapped in the underground operations room at the RAF's HQ in northwest London. At the same time General de Gaulle was recording a broadcast for the

BBC. He'd first agreed to do this on 4 June, but changed his mind on the 5th after discovering Eisenhower's own pre-recording would not be mentioning him. He'd finally been persuaded to cooperate at 4 a.m. on the 6th. Meanwhile, devoid of news, the BBC's midday bulletin began with the words: 'No details have yet come in from the Allied side of the progress of the operations.'

Midday – 2 p.m: Turning point on the beaches

By midday the American soldiers on Utah were advancing beyond flooded fields behind the beach in search of the US paratroopers who'd dropped a few miles inland. Utah marked the western edge of the entire operation, and the troops landing there occupied a vulnerable spot on the coast. Shortly after midday they made contact with the paratroopers of the US 101st Airborne Division in a rendezvous that was one of the key moments on the Allies' right flank.

As more Allied units were thrown into the assault, progress was being made on all five beaches. Even on Omaha, ground was being captured – a few platoons were assembling on the ridge and the village of Vierville had been taken. But most men were still pinned down beneath the sea wall and the tide was advancing ever closer towards them. Faced with the threat of being pushed back into the sea, the troops

were forced to inch forward, and they fought to cling on to every advantage they could seize.

By 12 p.m. Franz Gockel, the 18-year-old German corporal, had been firing his machine-gun almost continuously for more than six hours. Throughout the morning he'd watched as US soldiers desperately tried to crawl towards whatever cover they could find, and he saw at least two of the enemy's landing-craft torn apart by mines. But here and there, more and more GIs had begun to reach the slopes of the bluffs, and at 1.30 p.m. Lieutenant General Bradley was told greater numbers of troops were now making their way up towards the ridge.

As the Americans came closer, Gockel realized that their fire was becoming more accurate. At one stage his gun jammed, and as he took his finger off the trigger to clean the dirty ammunition belt, bullets flew in though his bunker's firing slit, hitting the weapon that had been in his hands only seconds before. He couldn't believe how lucky he'd been to escape injury.

Behind Gold Beach British troops were slowly moving southwest towards Bayeux. Beyond Juno the Canadians were striking out in the direction of Caen, despite the loss of scores of landing-craft carrying armour that was due to support them. Only six out of their 40 tanks reached the shore. Inland their progress was slowed by heavy street-fighting in Courseulles, but the Canadians' second-wave units were able to push beyond the battle and maintain the advance.

Midday – 2 p.m: The road south

At noon, a mile behind Sword Beach, the KSLI were preparing to head towards Caen. They were due to ride on Sherman tanks, but the vehicles had failed to arrive. The battalion's commanding officer made his way back to the chaos on the beach and saw that the tanks were still snarled up in traffic jams. There was nothing for it but to walk, and Captain Eaves helped map out a route heading directly south.

Three miles to their left, the commandos who'd landed with the first wave had been making swift progress towards the British airborne troops, who'd been holding Pegasus Bridge since the small hours. Marching to the sound of Lord Lovat's personal piper, they reached the bridge shortly after midday. The commandos then crossed the river in search of the units who were holding the Allies' extreme eastern flank, including Lieutenant Colonel Otway's 9th Parachute Battalion.

After landing on Sword, Doon Campbell had managed to scribble a few words describing conditions on the front line. Rushing down to the water's edge in search of a landing-craft, the Reuters correspondent paid a crewman £5 to take the report to England. While making his way back up the beach, he passed many bodies and later wrote that some were 'only half-dead, their blood clotting in the sand'.

Campbell crept to a ditch beyond a cratered road and tried to thumb a lift from armoured cars heading towards the town of Ouistreham. The Allies were pushing further and further south, and he'd have to move on if he was to witness the advance. So far he'd only seen events on the beach and he was keen to discover what was happening beyond the coast, in Caen and elsewhere.

TOP-SECRET

Morale in the front line

By 1944 many battalions in the British Army had not seen action for four years. The fact that some units were sent to the front line time and again while others were kept at home was for Churchill a 'painful reflection'. As D-Day approached, any feelings of frustration were forgotten and an air of eager anticipation was common among many Allied troops. Most felt they were at their peak of physical fitness and training, and this was reflected in a general enthusiasm to get the job done.

For thousands of soldiers, their first day in Normandy was their first day in battle, and most found they had much to learn. Junior officers were as inexperienced as their men, and initially scores of them were picked off by snipers. In the days to come they removed their badges of rank and other telltale signs, such as pistols and binoculars.

Many Allied troops were shocked to find that the much-vaunted Nazi super-soldiers were men just like them. In the first weeks of the campaign, some even found unexpected weaknesses in German tactics. One British lieutenant wrote that German soldiers 'encourage the myth that although superior as fighting men, they were beaten only by numerically greater forces. In my experience this was not so.'

Many Germans clung on to their army's high reputation built during the blitzkriegs of 1940. But reality had moved on. Units battered by the Russians were sent to France to rest, and by 1944 their numbers were often replenished with all that Hitler had left: old men and boys. No soldier could fail to notice that the Luftwaffe - the German Air Force - had largely been driven from Normandy by Allied air superiority, and many found the absence of air support a constant irritation.

Unlike the 'sub-human' Slavs, the Allies were regarded by German soldiers as a more humane opponent, and the troops in France rarely fought with the fanatical devotion shown by the Nazis in the east. After years of tranquillity, some units were less than prepared for the rigours of war, and others were distracted by the growing hostility of the local population. But what sapped morale most of all was the unavoidable realization that Germany simply couldn't win the war.

Bomb damage in Caen

2 p.m. – 4 p.m: Nowhere to hide

The carnage in Caen wasn't restricted to the prison. As a key German strongpoint, the city had frequently been the target of Allied air raids, and at 1.30 p.m. the bombers returned once again. The latest attack destroyed many buildings in the centre of the city, including the much-hated Gestapo HQ. But it was empty, its occupants having fled just an hour or so before the raid, taking with them a new list of the most important Resistance volunteers being held at Caen prison.

André Heintz had been sheltering in a cellar, but when bomb blasts blew open the door, he rushed to the city hospital where his sister was a nurse. He joined an ambulance crew and, with bombs still falling, helped search for survivors trapped beneath piles of rubble. On returning to the hospital, he heard that a bomb had exploded in the grounds, burying a nurse. The next blast had freed her, leaving her dumbfounded as to how she'd survived. André realized he needed to identify the building as a hospital, so, taking buckets of blood from the operating theatres, he

stained four sheets and spread them into a red cross. It was spotted by a reconnaissance aircraft, which waggled its wings in recognition.

The bombers were aiming to soften the defences of Caen in support of the approaching British troops. But the soldiers advancing from Sword were unaware that they'd already been spotted by the gun-crews of enemy howitzers, which were dug in on a ridge near the village of Periers-sur-le-Dan. As Bob Littlar, Bill Farmer and Gisser Owens made their way up the slope, they were moving into range. Soon shells began to fall

around them, and the KSLI realized that their first battle of D-Day was about to begin.

The battalion was split into four companies – W, X, Y and Z – each consisting of around 120 men, and an HQ company, which included Captain Eaves. The companies moved close enough to each other to be able to offer mutual support, yet still retained some distance to avoid presenting an easy target to enemy machine-gunners. At 2 p.m. the men of Z Company were sent east towards the Periers-sur-le-Dan battery, leaving the rest of the KSLI to push south.

2 p.m. – 4 p.m: Walking into danger

The road the KSLI were following wound steadily up a slope towards Beuville and Biéville. The closer the men got to the two villages, the harder the Germans fought to hold them back. Snipers tried to pick off the British officers, occasional mortar bombs scattered the troops, and here and there an unseen German machine-gun would instantly send the men diving for cover.

Approaching Beuville on the inside of a bend, Bob Littlar couldn't see what lay ahead. Walking on either side of the road the troops moved cautiously, their tired and blackened faces already showing the strain of battle. Gisser Owens was on the outside of the bend and had a clear view of the landscape in front of him – but this gave the Germans ahead a clear view of him too.

Suddenly a sniper opened fire, sending a bullet into the ammunition belt Owens was wearing round his neck. It exploded with such force that he was left with no chance of survival. There was no time to bury him – that would be done by the troops following behind the KSLI – and there was no time to grieve. Bob Littlar and Bill Farmer were constantly aware of the threat of danger and the permanent need to be prepared for whatever might be around the next corner.

At the start of the morning around 40 German tanks had advanced on the east side of the river Orne. But once the extent of the seaborne invasion had become clear, they'd been brought back across the river by General Marcks.

By 2 p.m. they were moving westwards along the northern edge of Caen. An hour later they'd stopped on a ridge and had taken up position in a wood near the village of Lébisey, facing towards the beaches 6 miles away. Between the KSLI and their main objective, a solid line of tanks now lay hidden in woodland.

As the KSLI marched south, the young soldiers were distracted by the plight of many of the local farm animals. Dead and wounded horses lay on the ground, having been caught in the overnight air raids, and everywhere cows that had not been milked were in obvious pain. As the men moved through Beuville towards Biéville, at around 3.30 p.m., they shot some of the animals to relieve their suffering.

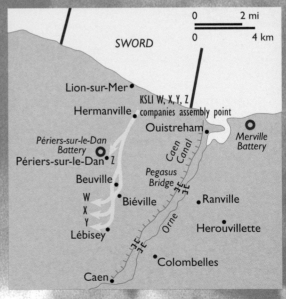

Map showing the advance south of the KSLI

3 p.m: Seizing the initiative on Omaha

On Omaha the US troops were building momentum in their struggle to send a significant number of men to the top of the slopes. The GIs were seizing more of the bluffs behind the beach, and had put several German machine-guns out of action. Fresh US soldiers were still landing, whereas the German machine-gunners were not being replaced and as the day wore on many were approaching exhaustion. Realizing that he'd not eaten for more than 18 hours, Gockel knew that if he was to continue defending his part of the beach he'd have to find some food.

He crept out of the back of his machine-gun position and made his way up a zigzag trench into a bunker, where he grabbed bread, sausage meat and milk. Some time later, at around 3 p.m., he began heading back to his post. Descending the slope, Gockel saw with alarm that US troops had exploited his absence and were climbing up beyond his bunker. He tried to turn round just as the GIs opened fire, but before he could escape bullets smashed into his hand, nearly severing three fingers. Reeling in pain, Gockel ran back towards other bunkers beyond the beach in search of other members of his unit.

Fifty miles to the east, the KSLI were advancing through the countryside past Biéville. Snipers initially made it too dangerous to march through the middle of the village, but by the time the battalion reached Biéville's southern edge, the snipers had melted away into the cornfields. As the rifle companies paused, Captain Eaves assessed their position. They were 4 miles from Caen, and all that stood in their way was the village of Lébisey. It appeared to be just as insignificant as Biéville.

CHAPTER NINE

DIGGING IN
D-DAY 4 P.M. – MIDNIGHT

By the middle of the afternoon a cautious confidence was growing among Admiral Ramsay, Air Chief Marshal Leigh-Mallory and many of the other Allied commanders. Except Ike. As the supreme commander waited in the war-room at Southwick House, anxiety and frustration bubbled just beneath his calm exterior. The first reports of the difficulties on Omaha had finally got through, and he'd learnt that hours after landing the troops were still pinned down. With the situation beyond his reach, Eisenhower felt powerless.

Senior officers on Omaha had called for air attacks to help clear the way, but precise targets couldn't be given to the US and British squadrons. No aircraft were scrambled and little was being done at the highest level to ease the plight of the men. Ike wanted to know what General Montgomery, the commander of the ground troops, was doing to improve things.

General Montgomery

Eisenhower's aides sensed that he wished he was running Monty's 21 Army Group himself – but he knew it was impossible to step in.

Montgomery was expecting to sail for Normandy that afternoon. With the operation taking place more than 100 miles from his HQ, he wanted to get to the battlefield as soon as possible. Monty wasn't the only ground commander who at that moment was more than 100 miles from the front line. Tense and worried, Rommel kept urging his chauffeur to drive faster, his adjutant Captain Lang later remembered. La Roche-Guyon was still a long way off and the field marshal interrupted his journey through France to telephone Speidel for the latest information. The news wasn't good.

By 4 p.m. key developments had begun to tilt the battle for the bridgehead in the Allies' favour. On the extreme eastern flank the troops who'd landed by sea earlier that day were already starting to push east across the river Orne. After crossing Pegasus Bridge, Lord Lovat's commandos had marched 2 miles before stumbling across a band of 75 exhausted para-troopers. The remaining men of the shattered 9th Parachute Battalion had reached the village of Le Plein, but they lacked the strength and ammunition to capture it alone. Lieutenant Colonel Otway agreed to provide support for the commandos as they mounted an attack themselves.

Otway had not been able to destroy the guns at Merville, but they'd been damaged and he knew the gunners had either been killed or captured. He felt he'd put the weapons out of action and that his mission had been completed.

But while Otway had been waiting for the commandos, the commander of the Merville Battery, Lieutenant Steiner, had inspected his guns and found that they were in much better condition than he expected; at least one could be fired by the troops who'd since joined him from a neighbouring unit. While the commandos attacked Le Plein, 2 miles away Steiner slipped back into his control bunker and ordered the guns to aim at the lock on the Caen Canal. At around 4 p.m. he gave the order and the Merville Battery opened fire.

4.30 p.m: The push for Caen finally falters

By 4 p.m. the KSLI had moved beyond Biéville, and Captain John Eaves knew they were now less than 4 miles from Caen. A temporary HQ had been set up in the centre of the village, and the battalion's commanding officer, his radio operators, aides and Eaves' six-man intelligence section were together mapping the progress of their soldiers. The 120 troops of Z Company were still caught up in a tough firefight at the Periers-sur-le-Dan gun battery, which had earlier threatened to block the KSLI's advance. In the middle of the afternoon they reported that the battle was in danger of sliding into a bloody stalemate.

Meanwhile, after bypassing the snipers in Biéville, the other three companies were now heading into the countryside. At 4.15 p.m. 200 KSLI soldiers were advancing down into the valley between Biéville and the Lébisey ridge. Furthest ahead were the men of Y Company, under the able command of Major Peter Steel, who was now forging further south into Normandy than any other Allied officer. Seeing the summit of a wooded hill ahead, Steel decided to halt once he was among the trees.

A mile further back Captain Eaves and the battalion's senior officers were gathered around their radio operators. By 4.30 p.m. news was coming in from all directions. While a handful of British Sherman tanks had finally caught up with the KSLI, 2 miles away the troops fighting at Periers-sur-le-Dan had found they were shooting at Poles who'd been forced to fight by the Germans. When one of the Poles escaped, he showed the KSLI a way in through the battery's defences.

Suddenly, at around 5 p.m., radio messages from Y Company came through to battalion HQ reporting a disaster. Major Steel had reached the wooded ridge near Lébisey and found machine-gunners hiding among the trees. Leading an attack, he had stormed forward into a hail of bullets and had been killed before he reached the enemy position. Steel's second in command had taken over and was radioing for instructions, but the battalion's HQ was preoccupied by a new threat. Taking the British by surprise, the tanks of the German 21st Panzer Division had emerged from their positions in the woods and were advancing down the side of the hill.

While Y Company was pinned down by machine-guns, 500 yards away 20 tanks were rolling towards Corporal Littlar, Private Farmer and the troops of X Company. In Biéville Eaves no longer needed to gather details by radio – he could hear the action for himself. The British tanks quickly moved into position and, supported by the anti-tank guns of the KSLI, fired at the approaching Germans. Four of the panzers were destroyed. The smoking wreckage blocked the German advance, and the rest of the panzer crews were forced to retreat.

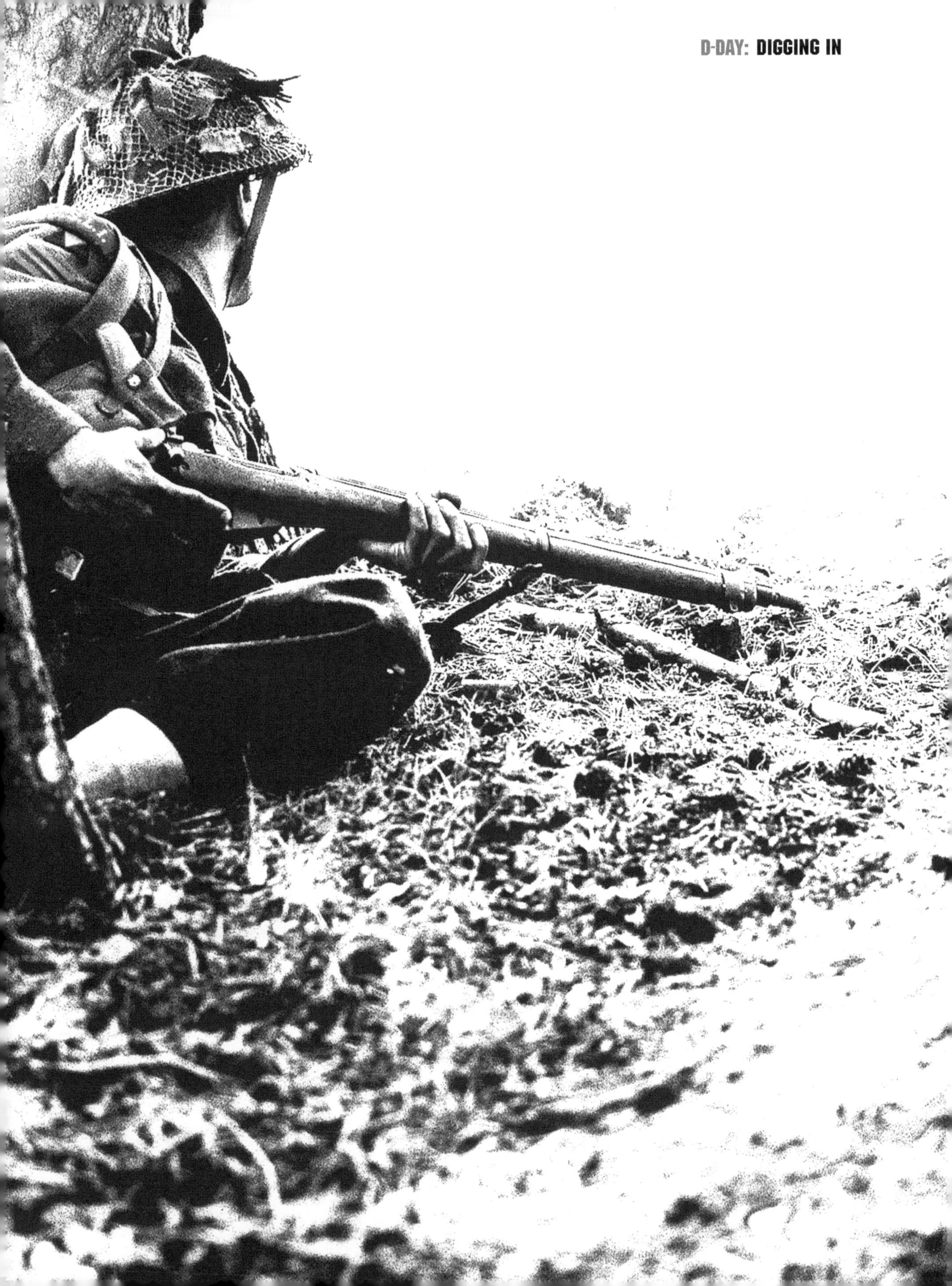

Later the German tanks targeted other British positions, but were outgunned and another nine were destroyed. In the woods at Lébisey General Marcks, who'd been in direct command of 21st Panzer Division since 8.45 a.m., had personally witnessed the battle against the British Shermans. Seeing that the attack had failed, Marcks ordered another column of tanks to push north towards the sea, warning it was up to them to stop the Allied advance or the battle of Normandy would be lost. As British troops continued to land on Sword, the forward units of 21st Panzer Division – unseen and undisturbed – steadily approached the coast. The young soldiers of the KSLI had already arrived, but thousands like them were still due to wade on to the beach, where they'd be exposed and vulnerable.

5 p.m: The horror resumes at Caen prison

In Caen prison the prisoners were in no doubt that the Allies were on their way. The waves of low-flying aircraft overnight, the sound of the naval guns at dawn and the heavy bombing raids they'd heard that afternoon convinced them that liberation was near. The captured Resistance volunteers knew their own fate remained unclear, but they took comfort from the hope that Allied troops were approaching their city: it was simply a question of when they'd arrive.

The Gestapo's HQ had been bombed, but the much-feared security agents had escaped to Falaise. Unharmed, they were still in a position to wield power. They wanted to stop their most important Resistance prisoners falling into Allied hands, but as they'd discovered overnight, it was impossible to move the volunteers out of Caen. After the morning's shootings, the Gestapo wasted little time in telephoning the prison to give the

commandant a new list of names. The executions at Caen prison weren't over.

Late in the afternoon the men, locked in their cells, once again heard the ominous sound of boots as guards marched along the passageways, opening doors and barking orders. Specific prisoners were summoned on to the landings, then pushed into small groups. The volunteers didn't know that outside the city the Allies' advance had foundered on the slopes of Lébisey – nor did they know that inside the prison armed men were again taking up position in the courtyard. Suddenly Robert Douin's name was shouted out.

Douin had no choice. He left the relative safety of his cell, and, joining a group of men, shuffled along the prison's corridors. Once more, gunfire could be heard and Douin – the proud father, artist and teacher – couldn't have been in any doubt about what awaited him as he followed the line of condemned prisoners into the bloodstained courtyard. The horrifying sight of orderlies shifting bodies in the afternoon sunshine told its own tale. He took his turn – and shut his eyes. A moment later, Douin's body was carried away to be laid with the others.

6 p.m: Battered, but holding on

By 6 p.m. the Allies were finally able to feel confident that they'd secured the bridgehead – at least until the panzer divisions threatened to arrive. The troops hadn't yet seized the sizeable chunk of Normandy their commanders had hoped for, but they were in France, they were holding what little ground they had and they weren't being pushed back into the sea.

Aid stations were treating injured men on the beaches, re-examining wounds that had been hastily looked at by the medics who'd accompanied each wave of assault troops. On Sword, the medics weren't the only help that had been available during the day. Jacqueline Bernard, a 23-year-old Frenchwoman from Hermanville, had been tending the wounded since dawn. A Red Cross assistant, she'd gone to the beach as soon as the operation had begun. In fact, she spent the whole of D-Day on Sword, and many soldiers must have looked on in disbelief as she dodged the mortars and shells.

Women also helped injured men on Omaha after Lieutenant Vivian Sheridan and other nurses of the 48th Surgical Hospital were sent to the beach in the late afternoon. There'd been no plans to put nurses in the front line on D-Day, but they were ordered in after the unit was told that the wounded were 'piling up on the beach'. Having been told to make her way through the surf using a body as protection, Vivian grabbed the remains of a red-haired boy who'd been no more than 20. He reminded her so much of her brother that she found the experience the most harrowing moment of the four invasions she took part in during the Second World War.

By 6 p.m. Franz Gockel's comrades had taken the injured machine-gunner away from the fighting on Omaha. He was driven to an aid post in the rear, where his maimed hand could be properly dressed. As Gockel left the front line, senior US commanders, accompanied by new waves of troops, were making their way on to the beaches where the horrifying debris of the nine-hour battle was evident for all to see.

Meanwhile, the first ships loaded with wounded were already preparing to sail for England. Among them was the USS *Samuel*

Chase. Slumped on a stretcher and suffering from exhaustion, photographer Robert Capa had woken up. As he lay surrounded by badly wounded men, he was painfully aware that he'd left the beach as soon he'd wanted to without having fired a shot in support of the operation. In fact, as a war correspondent, Capa was not allowed by international law to take part in the fighting. But that didn't stop his mind filling with guilt. When the man next to him woke to find himself on a hospital ship, he looked at Capa and described himself as a coward. Capa replied that if either of them was a coward, it wasn't the soldier.

In London, picture editor John Morris was waiting for the first images that would truly capture the horrors of D-Day. Shots from other photographers were available, but none was what he wanted to see – pictures that would make him feel as if he was actually there. Nine hours after the BBC had first broadcast news of the invasion there was still no official word on the troops' progress. There was nothing Morris could do to find out about the fate of his close friend Robert Capa, so he had no choice but to carry on waiting.

Previous page: US medics treating casualties on Omaha beach
Above: Horsa gliders after landing near the river Orne

8 p.m: Fending off the panzers

A few miles north of Morris's Soho office, Garbo was secretly in action once again. In the early hours of D-Day he'd sent a warning that could only have impressed the Germans. Garbo had since prepared an even more significant message, and this was radioed to Madrid at 8 p.m. Exploiting his previous reports, which exaggerated the number of Allied troops, Garbo warned Madrid that other major invasions were still being planned. Normandy appeared to be no more than a diversion.

Garbo's messages were designed to protect the Allied troops from the panzer divisions. But while his latest report was being sent to Madrid, the leading tanks of 21st Panzer Division managed to exploit the gap between the British

troops at Sword and the Canadians at Juno. They reached the coast at 8 p.m., opening up the way for the rest of the unit to follow on later.

Looking out at the vast fleet in the Channel, the panzer crews could see for themselves the immense scale of the enemy operation they were up against. Suddenly, just after 9 p.m., 250 Allied aircraft and gliders swept in low over the coast, bringing reinforcements to the British paratroop battalions east of the river Orne. Fearful that they were about to be trapped between fresh soldiers and the sea, the German tank crews quickly turned round and retreated towards Caen.

By 9 p.m. the Allies had stopped pushing south and were preparing to dig in for the night. Throughout the bridgehead, liberated French civilians were giving the troops food and drink –

British airborne troops digging in, with a glider in the background

especially the local apple brandy, calvados. The occasional lucky soldier was even offered a bed and clean sheets. Others made do with a spot in a barn. But the vast majority prepared to spend the night slumped in a shallow trench or crater beside the beaches and hedges of Normandy.

After being wounded at dawn, paratroop officer Lieutenant Alan Jefferson had spent the day lying on the floor of a farmhouse near the Merville Battery; he was still awaiting medical attention. At 6 p.m. the 9th Battalion's padre had arrived in a captured German vehicle and had taken four of the most severely wounded men to an aid post. At 9 p.m. the padre returned and picked up Jefferson and three other men. He drove back to the paratroopers' aid station, narrowly missing an ambush, and half an hour later Jefferson's wounded leg was being

treated. En route they passed close to Le Plein, where Lieutenant Colonel Otway, Private Sid Capon and the rest of the 9th Parachute Battalion were digging in for the night.

11 p.m: Counting the cost

The men of the KSLI's Y Company were still trying to pull back to a safer position. Stuck on the slopes beneath the village of Lébisey, the 120 soldiers had been pinned down by enemy machine-gunners for six hours. At 11 p.m., as darkness closed in, X Company was ordered to move up to the vulnerable area. Supporting each other, the two groups made their way back to battalion HQ at Biéville. As the troops retreated, the senior officers in Biéville were told that Z Company had finally captured the gun battery at

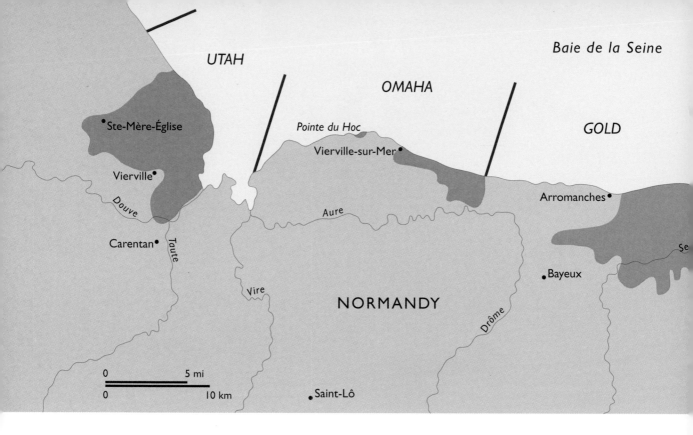

Periers-sur-le-Dan. They'd been fighting since 2 p.m. and had lost nine men.

Altogether, the KSLI suffered 113 casualties among the battalion's 600 soldiers who reached France on D-Day. The regimental diary described this as 'not as severe as expected'. Of the 29,000 British troops who landed on Sword Beach on 6 June, 1200 were killed or wounded during the course of the day. This amounts to a casualty rate of around 4 per cent, which was significantly lower than had been predicted. The rates for Juno and Gold were around 7 per cent and 4 per cent respectively. For Utah it was 0.8 per cent.

Nowhere was the scale of destruction greater than on Omaha. At one point Lieutenant General Bradley feared that of the 34,250 men who landed on the beach on D-Day, around 66 per cent had been killed or wounded. This figure is undoubtedly too high, but the true casualty rate has never been precisely determined. Con-servative estimates have said there were as few as 2000 casualties, but the truth is probably

closer to at least 5000. Omaha has since come to be considered as one of the most painful ordeals the Allies suffered in the latter part of the war.

It was a tragedy that couldn't have been easily averted. The German troops who'd been manning the defences on Omaha were of only average ability, but they'd been supported on 6 June by the far more able men of the 352nd Infantry Division. This unit had been temporarily operating near the beach – not due to the genius of Rommel, but through a chance training manoeuvre. Figures for the number of German casualties on D-Day have not been confirmed, but by 30 June Rommel's Army Group B had lost 80,783 men.

It was feared that losses among the airborne forces would reach a devastating level of around 70 per cent – or so the commander-in-chief of the Allied air forces had warned in an official protest sent to Eisenhower before D-Day. Although Leigh-Mallory's pessimistic expectations proved to be unfounded, the casualty rate was still around 17 per cent. Late on D-Day he sent an apology to Ike, accepting that his

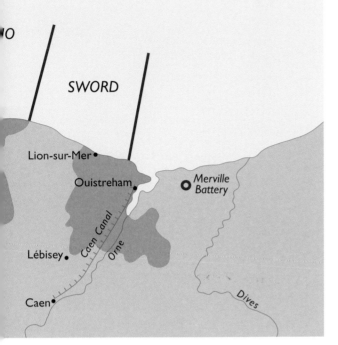

Map showing Allied positions at midnight on D-Day

warnings had been misguided and insisting that he had never had 'greater pleasure in admitting he was wrong'. That evening Eisenhower was preparing for the inspection voyage he was due to make to the waters off the beaches the following day.

Midnight: Rommel prepares to take charge

Rommel finally got back to his HQ at around 9.15 p.m. When his car pulled up at La Roche-Guyon, loud music could be heard coming from Speidel's office and Rommel's aide commented on this briefly to the chief of staff. 'Do you honestly believe,' Speidel replied, 'that my listening to Wagner will make any difference to the course of the invasion?' He and Rommel vanished into an office and at last the field marshal felt he could finally begin to impose his mark on the battle. For the next few hours he began to prepare for the coming campaign.

By the time Speidel had finished updating Rommel, it was abundantly clear that the operation was more than a local assault. This was

clearly an invasion. But still neither man believed that this was the main invasion, and both were confident in their ability to halt the Allies' advance and force a defeat or at least a stalemate that would allow Germany to negotiate the future direction of the war.

As far as the KSLI and the rest of the assault troops were concerned, the future course of the war was only going to go one way. It was true that by midnight the Allies had failed to seize major objectives, including Caen, and neither had they built a single 50-mile front uniting all five beaches. But they'd broken through the enemy's defensive line within 24 hours, and had inflicted a blow from which the Germans were never to recover.

Late that night Eisenhower's HQ issued its second communiqué, and at midnight the BBC announced: 'Reports of operations show our forces succeeded in their landings.' After four years, the Allies had finally returned to the northern shore of occupied Europe.

'Call from Monty, 7 pm, the Germans are surrendering, North and West Germany, Holland, Denmark and Norway ... the news of the surrender was announced at 8 pm on the BBC'

Eisenhower's diary entry, 4 May 1945, written by Kay Summersby

EPILOGUE

In the months before D-Day many Allied commanders' plans focused on the capture of the coast, as if this, rather than progressing south, was their main objective. In some cases, this line of thought overshadowed preparations for the first few days of the campaign.

On the morning of 7 June the British were harshly reminded just how difficult the battle for Normandy would be. At 8.45 a.m. the 2nd Warwicks tried to capture Lébisey Woods, the scene of Major Steel's death the previous afternoon. But after taking many casualties, they retreated to the position held by the KSLI at Biéville, and here the two battalions were ordered to dig in for the following four weeks.

Subsequent criticism of the lack of Allied momentum in those first, vital days may be justified, and some of the British commanders were more guilty of this than their American counterparts. General Montgomery shifted the focus of the campaign to the west and the battle for the port of Cherbourg, which fell to US forces on 27 June.

Allied support troops advance through Normandy

Above: British troops march through Lébisey en route to Caen
Overleaf: Capa's shot of US troops pushing beyond Omaha. The vast invasion fleet is visible in the background.

After several false starts, Caen wasn't liberated until 19 July, and much of the subsequent battle to break out of Normandy was bloody and pro-tracted. The countryside, marked by sunken lanes and high hedgerows, could be easily defended and wasn't suited to offensive actions by tanks. But by August, using their air superiority, the Allies had eroded the panzer divisions to the point where they were able to reach open ground to the east.

On 15 August a second, smaller Allied force landed on the southern coast of France. Paris fell 10 days later, and in September the Allies advanced into Belgium and the Netherlands. As the harsh winter of 1944–5 began to bite, the Germans regrouped and launched their last major offensive in the west, pushing deep into Belgium.

In early 1945 the Allies regained the upper hand. They crossed the Rhine in March and, advancing through the heartland of Germany, they liberated concentration camps, seeing for the first time evidence of the Nazis' atrocities. The Allies continued moving east, but the Russians were the

TOP-SECRET

Shock and disbelief: the first pictures of Omaha

Throughout 7 June people on both sides of the Atlantic were still waiting for accurate details of the invasion. Picture editor John Morris knew he had to give shots to a courier by 9 a.m. on Thursday 8 June if they were to be included in the next issue of Life magazine. But by the early evening of the 7th Robert Capa's films from the front line had still not arrived at Morris's Soho office.

Morris didn't yet know it, but that morning Capa had arrived back at Weymouth aboard the troop-ship USS Samuel Chase and had sent his 10 rolls of films to London. When Morris finally received them at around 9 p.m. he passed them to a darkroom assistant - 16-year-old Dennis Banks - telling him to develop them as fast as he could. Banks put the pictures into a drying cabinet, turned up the heat and closed the doors. But the heat was too much. With the pictures beginning to melt the teenager, in tears, quickly asked Morris to see if any were salvageable.

Eleven frames could be rescued - they were grainy and some were a little blurred but there was no doubt that they captured the hour of the attack. At 3.30 a.m., less than six hours before the 9 a.m. deadline, Morris rushed round with them to the military censor's office and joined the queue. Growing ever more worried, he was delayed by the censor until 8.45 a.m. With just 15 minutes to reach the dispatch rider who'd be taking official documents to a waiting aircraft, Morris raced to Grosvenor Square and found the courier with just one minute to spare.

Capa's pictures of Omaha Beach on D-Day, published in Life magazine on 19 June, sealed his reputation as a world-class photographer. He himself returned to Omaha on 8 June and made his way to Bayeux. He learnt about the darkroom accident a week later, and Morris has since said that he took the news well: 'Capa was a gambler and knew that some you win, some you lose.'

first to enter Berlin. Fearing capture, Hitler committed suicide on 30 April.

With Germany's armies everywhere surrendering to local Allied units, the chief of staff (operations) of the German armed forces, Colonel General Jodl, met Allied officers outside Reims on 7 May. There he signed the instrument of surrender, which was signed on behalf of Britain by Lieutenant General Sir Frederick Morgan, the original planner of D-Day. Eleven months after the Allies landed in Normandy, Churchill and new US president Harry Truman declared 8 May VE Day – Victory in Europe Day. Cheering crowds thronged Piccadilly Circus and Times Square.

In the Pacific, however, the war was still dragging on, and the Allies developed plans to mount a second huge invasion – this time of Japan. But the idea was dropped after the atombomb attacks on Hiroshima and Nagasaki forced Japan to surrender on 14 August. The following day was named VJ Day – after six long years the Second World War had finally drawn to a close. Worldwide it had cost at least 50 million lives, of which more than 25 million were civilians.

The political map of eastern Europe was altered for half a century, and for years this prompted the Allies to maintain a military presence in western Europe. The US 1st Infantry Division, which had landed on Omaha on D-Day, crossed France and entered Germany in 1945. It's still there. The financial implications of the war lasted for decades.

For many of the survivors of Normandy the psychological toll will last for ever. Sixty years later, in discussing their stories, many of the veterans quietly told of recurring nightmares, guilt and other emotions that have haunted them since 6 June 1944.

Rémy Douin

Rémy Douin

When Rémy Douin came back to Caen in August 1944 he found the city in ruins. He and his mother tried to find out what had happened to his father, Robert, but it wasn't until the return of some of the prisoners who'd been sent to Germany that they were able to be certain. The bodies of the men who were massacred on D-Day were never found, and to this day Robert has no known grave.

Rémy began supporting his family immediately after the war, working in the civil service before later going into business. He believes that had things been different he could have followed the family tradition and become an artist. But the war and financial demands made that impossible.

Bernard Duval

André Heintz

Today he lives in Caen where he gives talks to schoolchildren on the work of the Resistance. Every year the families of those killed in the Caen prison massacre hold an annual memorial service at the prison on 6 June, and Rémy's mother attended as often as she could until her death in 1982.

Bernard Duval

On 4 June Bernard Duval was transported by train from the Compiègne camp, 45 miles away from Paris, to Germany. He was one of thousands of Resistance prisoners from all over France who were pushed into cattle trucks and sent on a four-day journey without food or water. The summer heat drove some people to drink their own urine,

and others lost their minds. Several died. Bernard arrived at the Neuengamme camp near Hamburg, but was later moved to the infamous Sachsenhausen camp, where he worked in a tank factory. After months of forced labour under the harshest conditions, he was eventually liberated by the Russians on 26 April 1945. Bernard returned to Caen on 6 June 1945 and needed medical care for six months. Today he still lives on the outskirts of the city.

André Heintz

Between D-Day and 8 July, when British troops reached Caen, the city was bombed more than 26 times. Throughout that period André Heintz helped the overstretched hospital staff, and

Franz Gockel

although the bombing claimed many lives, he believes that most of the population understood why the Allies were targeting their city. When Caen was finally liberated on 19 July André described it as the most 'beautiful day of my whole life'. After the war he taught French at Edinburgh University until 1947, when he returned to Caen to teach French as a foreign language. He did this until 1983 and still lives in the city.

Jacqueline Bernard
One of the most surprising moments on Sword Beach was the arrival of Jacqueline Bernard, the 23-year-old French Red Cross assistant, who spent the day by the water's edge helping injured troops. Three weeks after D-Day she met a British officer, Captain John Thornton, whom

she married in 1945. They settled in Normandy. Jacqueline died in 2002.

Corporal Franz Gockel
When Corporal Franz Gockel was shot in the hand he was sent first to the village of Colleville and then to Paris. After he recovered from his wound, he was again in action until captured by the Americans in the Vosges in November 1944. After the war, Gockel came to know some of the former GIs who'd landed on Omaha on D-Day, and has received an award for the understanding and goodwill he's since tried to build. Many of his comrades at Omaha – most of whom were younger than 20 – lie buried among the 21,500 graves in the German cemetery at La Cambe. Today he lives in Hamm in northwest Germany.

Lieutenant General Dr Hans Speidel
During the summer of 1944 Speidel was dismissed from his post as chief of staff of Army Group B but was not told why. On 6 September he visited Rommel at Herrlingen, and the next day he was arrested at home. Speidel was associated with the defeatism that Rommel himself had been accused of, and was held prisoner for seven months before escaping. After the war, he worked with NATO, becoming commander of Allied Land Forces in Europe from 1957 to 1963. He died in 1984.

Field Marshal Erwin Rommel
On 17 July 1944 two RAF fighter-bombers flying over Normandy strafed a black staff car that had been caught on an open road near Vimoutiers. Inside, Rommel suffered serious head injuries,

and in August he returned home to Herrlingen to recover. Three days after Rommel was hurt, anti-Hitler conspirators exploded a bomb that wounded the Führer but failed to kill him. Anyone implicated in the attack was quickly rounded up and executed, and suspicion fell on many people, including Rommel. On 14 October two generals visited his home and gave him the choice of a traitor's trial or suicide. Rommel opted for the latter. He was given a state funeral and his ashes were buried in Herrlingen. He was 53.

Field Marshal Gerd von Rundstedt

The German commander-in-chief west, Field Marshal von Rundstedt, was captured in 1945. He was taken to Britain, where he was accused of war crimes, but the investigation was dropped because of his poor health. Von Rundstedt was held in captivity until 1949, and after his release he lived in Hanover until his death in 1953.

Robert Capa and John Morris

John Morris left *Life* magazine in 1946 and eventually became the executive editor of the Magnum photo agency, which Capa and four others founded in 1947. In 1954 Capa was asked to cover an assignment in Vietnam. After taking a picture of French soldiers, he stepped on a Vietminh landmine near Doaithan and died a short time later. He was 40 years old. John Morris now lives in Paris, which he describes as Capa's city; it was there that Morris last saw Pinky in 1953. He says Paris makes him think of Capa almost every day.

Jean and Jay Cain

Officially, 749 men were killed during Exercise Tiger, but personnel lists have been lost, so it is possible that the true figure is closer to 1000. Jay Cain's body was never found, and he is commemorated at the US military cemetery in Cambridge, UK, where his name is included on a wall dedicated to 5126 US personnel listed as missing in action. His twin brother Jean returned home in 1945 and worked as a salesman for Coca-Cola. He lives in Missouri.

Coxswain Joe 'Eddie' McCann

Eddie McCann, the 15-year-old boat coxswain, spent nearly two months ferrying troops and supplies to the beaches after D-Day. When he returned to the United States, aged 16 and the veteran of four invasions, he volunteered for extra-hazardous duty with US Navy special forces and was sent for training in Florida. It was there

Eddie McCann

that he met his wife Helen, and today they live near where Eddie grew up in Washington State. Among other things, he became a traffic policeman in California, and while attending a road accident, he was deliberately knocked down by a drunk driver. Although he still suffers a permanent degree of pain, he remains tireless in his campaign to increase public understanding of the horror of Exercise Tiger.

Commander Skahill and Lieutenant Doyle

Commander Bernard Skahill retired from the navy in 1947 and moved to Seattle, where he worked for Boeing. He never spoke openly about Exercise Tiger. Within the US Navy, Skahill was initially unfairly identified with the large loss of life, but this view softened with time, and three admirals attended his funeral when he died in 1966, aged 68. Admiral Don Moon, who commanded the naval side of the exercise, never got over the scale of the tragedy. He became the disaster's last victim when, on 5 August 1944, he committed suicide.

After the war, John Doyle, the skipper who returned for the survivors, started a vending machine business in Montana. In 1989 he returned to Lyme Bay to mark the 45th anniversary of Tiger, and less than two months later he passed away, revered to the last by the men he saved that night. Always a quiet, modest man, he had a lifelong passion for the rugged country of his home state, and died during a fishing trip in the Bitterroot Mountains. He'd always said that since the fish in the mountain streams had fed him for so many years, his ashes should be scattered in the water in return.

Lieutenant Vivian Sheridan

Vivian Sheridan, the nurse who was sent on to Omaha, accompanied US troops all the way to Germany, where she treated survivors of the Dachau death camp. She later worked in front-line hospitals during the Korean War, before retiring from the army as a lieutenant colonel after 28 years' service.

General Dwight D. Eisenhower and Kay Summersby

The indisputable success of history's biggest military operation brought General Eisenhower enormous support and admiration, especially in the USA, where he was regarded as a genuine all-American hero. But heroes who rid the world of evil tyranny don't have mistresses – or at least that was the view in Washington at the time. When Eisenhower flew from Frankfurt to the USA in November 1945 he was forbidden to take Kay with him, and the two never spoke intimately again.

Kay was hurt at being suddenly cold-shouldered, although she came to understand the pressures Eisenhower was under. She tried to move on and took up new military postings, first in Berlin and a year later in the USA. In the course of her duties she occasionally met Eisenhower in Washington, but after a while she left the army and went to New York, where she married.

In 1974 Kay wrote of her wartime affair in her book *Past Forgetting*, based on the general's wartime diaries. It was her first chance to reveal the facts behind rumours that were still circulating decades after their affair had ended. Soon after the book was completed, Kay died in January 1975. In 2001 the diaries, containing entries by both Ike and Kay, were acquired by the US National Archives and have since been made available to the public.

Eisenhower leapt from an anonymous position as a lieutenant colonel in 1941 to five-star general in the space of just four years. After the war, he became the army chief of staff, then president of Columbia University, and from 1950 to 1952 he commanded NATO forces in Europe. He went on to serve as president of the United States for two terms, from 1953 to 1961, backing international alliances against the threat of communism. During part of this time the most senior soldier in NATO was Speidel. Eisenhower died in Washington in 1969.

Doon Campbell

Correspondent Doon Campbell covered the war in Europe up until VE Day. He subsequently worked in India, Burma, China, Palestine, Jordan, Vietnam, Cambodia and Iraq, and interviewed world leaders from Gandhi to Ho Chi Minh. He ended his 30-year career with Reuters as the agency's editor and deputy general manager. He died in May 2003, at the age of 83. Few of his achievements outshone the moment when, as the youngest British reporter covering D-Day, he landed on Sword Beach with Lord Lovat's commandos.

Lovat himself was wounded shortly after the invasion and later retired from the army to build up his family estates. He died in 1995.

Juan Pujol – Garbo

From start to finish, the story of Garbo is almost beyond belief. The trust the Germans placed in him was wholly genuine and wholly misplaced.

After D-Day, seven German divisions that the British feared would be sent to Normandy were held in the Pas de Calais for a fortnight. In fact, it wasn't until October that the Germans believed the First US Army Group (FUSAG) had finally been broken up. In reality, it had only ever existed on paper. For his unswerving loyalty, the Germans paid Garbo's entirely fictitious network a total of £31,000 – an enormous sum in 1945. He was also awarded the Iron Cross, which was normally never given to anyone who was not German. An exception was made in his case on the direct orders of Hitler.

Working for ideological reasons, Garbo never asked for cash, but was given £17,500 by the Allies and awarded the MBE. After the war, he returned to Spain, where he met the German case officer who for four years had been receiving his false letters and radio reports. The officer was desperately trying to find a place of safety away from the Allies, so he asked Garbo for help. Garbo promised to speak to his secret network.

After 1949 MI6 faked Garbo's death – not even his estranged wife knew he was alive – and he settled in Venezuela. It was there that the writer Nigel West found him in 1984 and brought him back to the UK to publicly receive his MBE and a toast at the Special Forces Club. He died in 1988. In 1945, Tomás Harris wrote a secret account of the entire case, which is now publicly available. Harris himself was killed in a car crash in Majorca in 1964. John Masterman, the chairman of the Twenty Committee, went on to become vice-chancellor of Oxford University, and in 1959 received a knighthood. Sir John died in 1988.

George Lane

Bob Littlar

Lieutenant George Lane

Lieutenant Lane, the commando captured while looking for secret mines, first heard about the invasion at 6 p.m. on 6 June in a prisoner-of-war camp in Germany. In 1945, while being moved to another camp, he managed to escape to Allied lines, and on his return to England he was awarded the Military Cross for his daring raids. George has always felt humbled by the luck he had during the war. Despite the considerable risks he undertook at the time – not least his frank conversation with Field Marshal Rommel – he survived and went on to make a name for himself in business on both sides of the Atlantic. Initially, George farmed his first wife's Northamptonshire estate before working in the financial markets of New York. He subsequently returned to the UK and now lives in London.

Corporal Bob Littlar and Private Bill Farmer

In the spring of 1945 the KSLI crossed the Rhine and reached the city of Bremen in northwestern Germany. After VE Day, Corporal Bob Littlar and Private Bill Farmer were told that they were due to join an advance guard that would be going to California ahead of the planned invasion of Japan. After the atom bombs were dropped, the pair were flown to the Middle East, where the KSLI and the rest of the 3rd Infantry Division were involved in policing Palestine. Bob and Bill both returned home when the division was disbanded

Bill Farmer

John Eaves

in June 1947. Bob subsequently worked for the Midland Bank and Bill became a lorry driver. Today they both live in Herefordshire.

Captain John Eaves

John Eaves, the KSLI's intelligence officer, suffered serious wounds to his legs and back after a mortar bomb exploded at his feet on 16 October 1944. The blast severed his achilles tendon, and he was sent back to England, where he spent a year with his left leg in plaster. He was never judged fit enough to return to his battalion, but was not demobbed until 1947. In 1950 he qualified as a solicitor and later ran his own law practice, first in Devon and then in Pembrokeshire, where he now lives.

Private Sid Capon

On 24 July Private Sid Capon was badly wounded by a mortar bomb and spent eight weeks recovering in hospital. He later returned to the battalion, and in May 1945 reached Wismar on the Baltic coast, where he encountered hardened Russian solders, many of them female. After VE Day the battalion was sent to India to prepare for action against the Japanese, but when the atom bombs brought an early end to the war, Capon was sent to Palestine, where he stayed until he left the army in April 1946. Sid trained as a builder and later set up a construction company. Today he lives in London and is very active in looking after the welfare of former members of the airborne forces.

Sid Capon

Alan Jefferson

Lieutenant Alan Jefferson

Alan Jefferson also left the army after the war, and for a while pursued his love of the theatre before turning his attention to writing, mostly about music and opera. He lives in Cornwall. Like many former members of the 9th Parachute Battalion, he occasionally returns to the Merville Battery to honour the memory of fallen comrades, including Lieutenant Mike Dowling. Dowling's body was found under lime trees near the battery and was buried at Bayeux. He was 34.

Over the years Jefferson got to know the battery's former commander Raimund Steiner, and the two still exchange regular letters. In 1944 Steiner and his men resisted all subsequent attacks by Allied troops and held out until 16 August, when they quietly slipped away, taking their guns with them. After the war Steiner returned to Austria, where he managed a sales department. Today he lives in Innsbruck.

Lieutenant Colonel Terence Otway

On 12 June 1944 Lieutenant Colonel Otway was injured by a shell blast. He suffered pain and headaches for weeks, and was evacuated on 19 July. After the war Otway wrote a history of the airborne forces' operations during the conflict, before leaving the army in 1948. In later years he ran a toyshop in Knightsbridge and sold life insurance to the senior men of Fleet Street, many of whom he got to know – including Doon Campbell. Today he lives in Surrey.

Terence Otway

Admiral Sir Bertram Ramsay and Air Chief Marshal Sir Trafford Leigh-Mallory

It is possible that Admiral Sir Bertram Ramsay's name would have become at least as familiar as Montgomery's had he survived the war, but he died in an air crash in January 1945. Air Chief Marshal Sir Trafford Leigh-Mallory became the highest-ranking RAF casualty of the Second World War when he too was killed in an air crash in November 1944.

General Montgomery

General Montgomery was promoted to field marshal in September 1944, and at the end of the war he was appointed commander-in-chief of the British Army of Occupation. In 1946 he became chief of the Imperial General Staff, and was granted the title of Viscount Montgomery of Alamein. He retired from the army in 1958 after 50 years' service. Montgomery's great strengths – not least his personal bravery, as demonstrated at Ypres – have never been disputed. Although it has been said of him that was he was unable to work as part of a team, his military successes and a genuine interest in his soldiers' well-being brought him the lasting respect of his troops. Viscount Montgomery died in 1976.

Lieutenant General Frederick Morgan

Lieutenant General Morgan was knighted in 1944. After retiring from the army in 1946 he later worked for Britain's atomic energy programme. He died in 1967. Modest, sincere and widely liked, Morgan planned three invasions that came to nothing, and a fourth that changed the history of the world.

In an operation that stretched the Allies to the limit, 156,000 troops captured a 50-mile stretch of coastline within 24 hours. They sustained 13,000 casualties, and at midnight on 6 June were holding some parts of the bridgehead only by a whisker. But they were secure enough to be able to launch a campaign that would ultimately end the war in Europe. The invasion was commanded by Eisenhower, who came to London just five months before it began. While he succeeded beyond all expectation, any attack on such a scale could never have been mounted had it not already been properly planned in detail. By virtue of his imagination, tenacity and patience, Lieutenant General Morgan's name surely belongs to D-Day as much as anyone's.

Sixty years on

Today the veterans of D-Day are in their 80s. Their memories of June 1944, which for some are as strong as if the events happened yesterday, still colour their speech and are clear in their eyes. Although most weren't seasoned fighters but civilians in uniform, they achieved things that make most of us pause in admiration. Some suffer from wounds that marked their time in France, others still carry shrapnel in their bodies, but many – though not all – bear no marked ill will towards the Germans.

In looking for the legacy of D-Day, talking to veterans is a natural place to start. But asking what they remember of their feelings at the time often prompts a similar response: 'I was too busy to think.' Anyone involved in D-Day was part of a huge machine. Serving on board a ship or living in the field gave a serviceman little chance to th   r act independently. Most wanted simply to co   ete the job at hand and go home to enjoy the peace and freedom they were fighting for. But, tough though military life was, few would deny that a political system that allowed individuals to take responsibility for their own actions was something worth fighting for.

For German soldiers serving a totalitarian regime there was little opportunity to act and think freely as we do today. Sixty years ago this freedom was something young men fought to uphold on the beaches of Normandy.

Right: The US cemetery at Omaha a year after D-Day
Overleaf: Omaha today

PICTURE CREDITS

BBC Worldwide would like to thank the following individuals and organizations for providing photographs and for permission to reproduce copyright material. While every effort has been made to trace and acknowledge copyright holders, we would like to apologize should there be any errors or omissions.

ABFM/Military Picture Library: p.102; BBC Archives: p.130; Bettmann/Corbis: p.22; © Dangerous Films, (photo Nick Gregory): p.136; © Dangerous Films, (photo Stephen F. Morley): pp.10–11 silhouette, 31, 17t, 26, 42, 45, 50, 51 silhouette, 57 silhouette, 61t, 62–3, 73r, 74, 78, 88, 107–8, 110, 112–13, 114–15, 121, 129, 131, 140–1, 144t, 146–7, 149–51, 156, 158–9; © Dangerous Films, (photo John Rogers): p.3c, 64–5, 67, 69, 110, 119, 120, 134–5, 144–5 silhouette, 145, 152–3, 161; D-Day Museum, Portsmouth: p.16, 80; D-Day Museum, Portsmouth/Courtesy Ordnance Survey: pp. 58–9, 82b, 92 backdrop; D-Day Museum, Portsmouth/U.S. Navy Photo: p.48; Defence Picture Library: p.86; Hulton: pp.28–9, 32, 34, 162–3; Imperial War Museum: pp.14–15, 17b, 18, 20–1, 25, 41, 44, 49, 61b, 66t, 71, 80–1, 82t, 84–5, 87, 90–1, 94–5, 100–1, 118, 124b, 127, 132–3, 138–9, 142–3, 148, 154–5, 164–5, 168–70, 184–5; Magnum Photos: p.137t; Mary Evans Picture Library: p.105; National Archives: pp.30–1, 33, 75, 106; PA Photos: p.8; Popperfoto.com: p.11, 46–7, 104; Reuters: p.66b; Robert Capa/Magnum Photos: pp.122–3, 172–3; Royal Naval Museum: p.93; Topham/ImageWorks: pp.186–7; Topham Picturepoint: p.55, 68; U.S. National Archives: pp.98–9; U.S. Naval Institute Photo Archive: p.52b.

All images of veterans are by courtesy of and the copyright of the veterans and their families.

INDEX